SUPERVISION

Sara Miller McCune founded SAGE Publishing in 1965 to support the dissemination of usable knowledge and educate a global community. SAGE publishes more than 1000 journals and over 800 new books each year, spanning a wide range of subject areas. Our growing selection of library products includes archives, data, case studies and video. SAGE remains majority owned by our founder and after her lifetime will become owned by a charitable trust that secures the company's continued independence.

Los Angeles | London | New Delhi | Singapore | Washington DC | Melbourne

SUPERVISION

A GUIDE FOR THE HELPING PROFESSIONS

CHRIS BECKETT

SAGE

Los Angeles | London | New Delhi
Singapore | Washington DC | Melbourne

SAGE

Los Angeles | London | New Delhi
Singapore | Washington DC | Melbourne

SAGE Publications Ltd
1 Oliver's Yard
55 City Road
London EC1Y 1SP

SAGE Publications Inc.
2455 Teller Road
Thousand Oaks, California 91320

SAGE Publications India Pvt Ltd
B 1/I 1 Mohan Cooperative Industrial Area
Mathura Road
New Delhi 110 044

SAGE Publications Asia-Pacific Pte Ltd
3 Church Street
#10-04 Samsung Hub
Singapore 049483

First published 2021

Editor: Kate Keers
Assistant editor: Ruth Lilly
Production editor: Martin Fox
Copyeditor: Jo North
Proofreader: Derek Markham
Indexer: Martin Hargreaves
Marketing manager: Camille Richmond
Cover design: Wendy Scott
Typeset by: C&M Digitals (P) Ltd, Chennai, India
Printed in the UK

Library of Congress Control Number: 2020937856

British Library Cataloguing in Publication data

A catalogue record for this book is available from the British Library

ISBN 978-1-5297-0073-2
ISBN 978-1-5297-0072-5 (pbk)

CONTENTS

LIST OF FIGURES AND TABLES

FIGURES

TABLES

ABOUT THE AUTHOR

Chris Beckett is now a freelance writer, but was for most of his working life a social worker, a social work manager and a social work lecturer. For many years, he has taught supervision on Continuing Professional Development courses attended by social work managers and senior practitioners, but also by managers from other professions such as nursing and occupational therapy. Chris is based in Cambridge, where he lives with his wife and several animals, and has three adult children and one granddaughter. In addition to writing a number of textbooks for social workers and human service professionals, he is the author of eight novels and three short story collections, and has won prizes for his fiction writing. He tries to apply his story-telling experience to his non-fiction books, in order to make them as lively and readable as possible.

INTRODUCTION
THE SCOPE OF THIS BOOK

This book has been written for two groups of people:

1 Managers, practitioner-supervisors and practice educators in social work agencies and other human service organisations who are engaged in supervising staff and students. (The term 'practice educator' is used here to refer to those who supervise students on placement: depending on the profession, this role may be referred to by other names such as 'mentor' or 'clinical educator'.)
2 Supervisees, particularly students and newly qualified practitioners, who want to understand what they should be able to expect from supervision, and what is expected of them.

The literature I cite in this book comes from many disciplines, including nursing, physiotherapy and medicine, and I also draw on work from the field of business and management. My own background is in social work, and most of my own examples will come from social work, but I believe this book should be relevant to supervisors, educators and supervisees in other human service organisations: for instance, in housing associations providing social care services, and in youth work agencies and mental health services in which relationship-based casework is a significant component of practice.

The book has developed out of teaching I have done over many years – mainly with social workers but also with people from other professions such as nursing – who are either moving into a role which involves taking supervisory responsibility for others, or have been performing that role for a while and are seeking to reflect on and develop their practice. I wanted to try and set down what I have learnt over the years from all those hours talking to supervisors, and from my own experience, in a previous career, of supervising a team of social workers over a ten-year period, latterly as the manager of a children and families team.

To some readers – experienced supervisors and experienced supervisees – much or most of what I say will already be familiar. If that applies to you, I hope you will not feel patronised by my going over things that you have already thought about. But in my experience, learning isn't just about being taught completely new things. I myself often find it helpful to unpack what I think I already *do* know – and perhaps know so well that I don't always think about it very much – and thus get a chance to re-examine and refine it a little, or even just restore my engagement with it. I hope you will feel the same on reading this book.

FOR SUPERVISORS AND PRACTICE EDUCATORS

The kind of supervision I address in this book is the kind that occurs in a human service organisation in which both accountability supervision and clinical supervision are necessary, and in which these are usually combined together. (I explain what I mean by this in Chapter 1.)

Supervision varies both between and within professions, and different kinds of supervision are indicated depending on the level of experience of the supervisee, but there are many general principles that apply across the board, whether the supervisee is a new and inexperienced student or a seasoned practitioner.

At the ends of chapters I will include 'Notes for supervisors'. These are aimed at all supervisors, including practice educators.

All supervisors are of course also supervisees themselves, and the way they supervise others will be influenced by the supervision they themselves are now receiving and have received in the past. So my comments addressed to supervisees are relevant to supervisors as well. (In fact, if you want to be a good supervisor, it's not a bad start to think about how you were – *and still are* – as a supervisee.)

FOR STUDENTS AND SUPERVISEES

There are two sides to supervision and the quality of the supervisory process depends on constructive input from supervisees as well as the input of supervisors. But supervision, as it is understood in professions such as social work, is not a concept that is necessarily familiar to everyone. This means that practice educators and those who supervise newly qualified staff need to bear in mind that supervisees will not necessarily understand what is needed from them. They may not know, for instance, that their own personal feelings are relevant and worth discussing, something that I explore in Chapter 5.

It also means that an introduction to supervision, such as this one, ought to address the needs of the supervisee as well as the supervisor. I am thinking in particular of students on placement, who are experiencing supervision for the first time, and of newly qualified workers, who may still be unsure about what they should expect of supervision, or what they should be bringing to it, though I hope that other supervisees will find this useful as well.

At the end of every chapter I will include 'Notes for supervisees', these are addressed to students but also to practitioners and indeed supervisors, who want to reflect on their needs and responsibilities as the recipients of supervision.

WHAT KIND OF BOOK THIS IS

This book draws on ideas from the literature, including research on supervision, but it is drawn more than anything else from experience: Firstly, my own experience as a supervisee, supervisor and educator, and secondly the experience of others, including the many excellent supervisors it's been my pleasure and honour to teach. I have also drawn extensively on the experience of my wife Maggie who has been supervising staff in the social work and social care fields for more than a quarter of a century – more than twice as long as my own experience in that role.

I have tried to make the book lively enough that it ought to be possible to read it through from one end to the other (it is also fairly short), but of course I am aware that most readers of text books dip into them rather than work through them, and the book is designed to work in that way also. This means that points are repeated a little more often than would be the case if I could be confident that people would read the book from beginning to end.

EXERCISES

As in my other books, I intersperse the text with 'exercises' or activities for the reader to consider. They could also be used for teaching purposes. Not all readers will want to spend time on these, but you do need to read through them as they are referred to in the subsequent discussion.

TERMINOLOGY

Gender

Most social workers in the UK, and most of the people who supervise social workers, are women. On the basis of my own teaching, I would say that the ratio is about 9 to 1, and I believe this is broadly consistent with national statistics. Women are in the majority in nursing, teaching and many of the other human service professions also. For this reason, I tend to refer to supervisees and supervisors as 'she' or 'her'. This is not intended to be disrespectful or dismissive of the male minority – of which, after all, I am a member.

Service users, customers or clients?

Fashions have changed over the years as to how to refer to the recipients of services and interventions from social workers and other human service professions. I use the terms 'service user' and 'client' interchangeably. I personally dislike the word 'customer', although I know it is widely used in adult social care, and I do not personally subscribe to the view that there is something stigmatising about the word 'client'. The truth is that none of these words really reflects the fact that the recipients of social work and other human services frequently do not have a choice in the matter. That absence of choice is one of the things that make good supervision particularly important in such services.

Cases

For the sake of brevity, I tend to talk about the material that a supervisee brings to supervision as her 'cases', though I know that not all supervisees will have their own allocated cases, and the word 'cases' may not necessarily be used at all in every context.

Clinical and accountability supervision (and other terms used for aspects of supervision)

In Chapter 1, I make a distinction between clinical supervision (between one professional and another) and accountability supervision (in which the supervisor is checking up on the work of someone in a subordinate position), as two distinct things that tend to be combined together in social work and other human services. I am not entirely happy with these terms, particularly the word 'clinical' with its medical connotations, but it is actually quite difficult to find words that do not have any other connotations at all.

The same applies to some of the other terms used in this book, such as 'Experience', 'Reflection' and 'Analysis' which I have borrowed from Jane Wonnacott (2012): these words too are not ideal, because they are used in a way that is somewhat different from their everyday meaning and that has the potential to cause confusion. But again, short of coining completely new words such as ... I don't know! ... 'Xagaz' or 'Plurque' (which would be fun but very hard either to remember or to take seriously!), there is really no way round this, and the reader will just need to bear in mind that words are often being used in a specific, specialist sense.

1

ACCOUNTABILITY SUPERVISION AND CLINICAL SUPERVISION

CONTENTS

There are two kinds of supervision ...

Well, actually that's not true. There are dozens of different kinds of supervision, depending on the personal, professional and organisational relationship between the supervisor and the supervisee, the organisation where it is taking place, the issue being discussed, the skills, personalities, training, beliefs and cultural assumptions of those involved etc. etc. However, there is a fundamental two-way split that runs through supervision, which it is important to be clear about from the start. I will call the two sides of this split *accountability supervision* and *clinical supervision*. This book is about supervision in contexts where both are necessary.

TWO KINDS OF OVERSIGHT

The term 'supervision' comes from words of Latin origin meaning 'over' and 'sight'. Supervision is oversight.

But there are different kinds of oversight. If you asked someone who worked in a factory what her 'supervisor' did, she might say something like 'it's someone who checks up on me and makes sure I'm doing my job properly'. If you asked a psychotherapist in private practice what her 'supervisor' did, she might say 'it's someone I reflect on my work with, someone who helps me disentangle my own feelings and history from those of my clients, someone I can brainstorm ideas with'.

The factory worker is talking about *accountability* supervision, which you'd expect to find in any organisation in some form or another (for how otherwise would organisations know whether their staff were doing what they were supposed to do?). It's a form of supervision that is about making sure that staff pull their weight and act appropriately, that guidelines are followed, targets met, appropriate guidance and training are provided and that problems with delivering the service are identified. The supervisor is overseeing the work of staff on behalf of the organisation.

The therapist, on the other hand, is talking about *clinical* supervision. Her supervisor is not her boss, is not 'above' her in a hierarchy, but a fellow-psychotherapist who the psychotherapist herself perhaps pays to provide this service, or perhaps receives from her on a reciprocal basis. What this kind of supervisor provides is distance, perspective, a second opinion. The supervisor isn't as emotionally involved as the therapist is and this means that, while there are many things about the therapist's clients she can't see (for she only knows about the client *through* the therapist), there will be things she notices that the therapist misses, for sometimes the therapist, in the midst of all the details and powerful feelings, 'won't be able to see the wood for the trees', or will find it hard to disentangle her own feelings from those of the client. So this kind of supervision is *also* oversight, but it is oversight from a position of relative detachment rather than from a higher position in a management hierarchy.

The factory worker may not need 'clinical' supervision in this sense, and the therapist in private practice does not need 'accountability supervision', but in social work agencies and similar human service organisations, *both* are essential (see Figure 1.1). So when we talk about good supervision, we are talking about a combination of both accountability *and* clinical supervision. If you look at the UK government's 'knowledge and skills statement for child and family practice supervisors' (DfE, 2018) you will see that the eight headings listed include both managerial and professional forms of skill and knowledge.

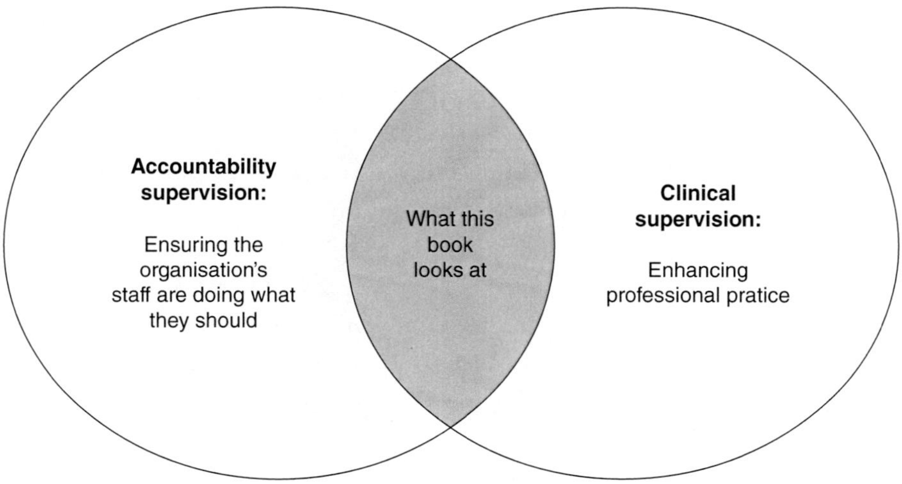

Figure 1.1 Accountability and clinical supervision

ACCOUNTABILITY SUPERVISION AND CLINICAL SUPERVISION

The reason we need both kinds of supervision in human service organisations, is that the work shares some of the characteristics of the work of a psychotherapist but not others. The similarities with the work of the psychotherapist are that the work is *relationship-based,* involves *distressing material,* and involves operating in *conditions of uncertainty*. The differences are that *service users don't have a choice,* the *organisation as a whole is accountable,* and *the organisation has to provide a service.*

Let us briefly unpick these:

The need for clinical supervision

- *Relationship-based work:* The relationship between the professional and the client is absolutely central to the whole endeavour. It's not like, say, the case of a garage mechanic, where it's helpful, no doubt, for the mechanic to have a good relationship with his customers, but the relationship is largely irrelevant to his ability to fix cars, and makes no difference to what he does when he's underneath the car with his tools. In social work, on the other hand, and in other human services, human interactions *are* the tools. But these tools are not like spanners. You can't just pick them up and put them down, they change over time, and they're affected by feelings.

- *Distressing material:* Human service professionals deal with things like child abuse, terminal illness, disability and dementia, and they must also deal with people who may be angry, hostile, grief-stricken, or mentally disturbed. Practitioners need to understand their own emotional responses if they are to be able to do their best for service users.
- *Conditions of uncertainty:* Human service workers do not usually operate in fields where there are simple, precise, technical answers. Their work takes place in what Donald Schön called 'The swampy lowlands, where situations are confusing messes incapable of technical solution … [but also] usually involve problems of greatest human concern' (Schön, 1983: 42). Practitioners' decisions may have huge consequences for other people's lives, but there is nevertheless no exact science to tell them what to do. Given the personal nature of the work, and the distressing emotions it stirs up (and the fact that the client's experience may have parallels with our own), it is important that human service workers have access to a form of supervision that will help them to disentangle what is going on, before reaching decisions about what to do.

The need for accountability supervision

- *Service users don't have a choice:* People can choose whether to go and see a psychotherapist, and can decide for themselves which therapist they want to see, but many of the clients of human service agencies have no choice but to work with professionals such as social workers, youth justice workers or community psychiatric nurses either because the professional is the only way of getting access to a service they need, or because there is some sort of legal requirement to do so. This places service users in a position where they have little power, and, in order to prevent misuses or abuses of that power, human service workers need to be accountable to someone other than themselves.
- *The organisation as a whole is accountable:* Human service workers are employed by organisations that are answerable to government and to the public. They can't just do whatever they feel like doing, or even whatever they think is important. They have to deliver the service that the organisation is mandated to deliver. Managerial oversight is needed to ensure that this happens.
- *The organisation has to provide a service:* Human service organisations can't determine their own workflow in the way that a therapist in private practice

> can, but have to offer a service to the whole community on the basis of need. They need to ensure that work is appropriately prioritised so that new work can be taken on, and that the time spent on each case is proportionate to that case's needs relative to the other work that needs to be done. These are matters that can't be determined by an individual practitioner, but require overview of workload of the team or work unit as a whole.

Bill McKitterick (2012: 23–4) speaks of 'two opposing forces', or two 'clusters' of forces. On one side is the 'cluster of forces of administration, managerialism and performance' and on the other the 'cluster of professionalism, thoughtful practice and relationship-based practice'. And these, he says, 'need to be reconciled in supervision as important, but *essentially distinct sets of activities, allowing neither to dominate or crowd out the other*. The real skill of the professional in this field, in both giving and receiving supervision, is to bring these forces together, using ... [the managerial/accountability side] to help deliver [the professional/clinical side]' (2012: 23. My italics).

MAINTAINING THE DISTINCTION

A small survey of social workers carried out by Turner-Daly and Jack (2017: 41) found that one third of respondents 'reported that supervision did not provide any opportunities for reflection, many of them indicating that meetings with their supervisors were exclusively focused on case management issues'. A study of supervision records by David Wilkins (2017), found that only a quarter of the records contained analysis (using the Department for Education's definition of that term [2015]). There was, for instance, 'little recorded attempt to explore why people might behave in certain ways or how different aspects of family life might interact to create or mitigate risk' (2017: 1135–6). Wilkins et al. (2017) looked at transcripts of supervision sessions in a 'children in need' social work team. A common pattern they identified was that an initial 'verbal deluge' of detail about a case (Wilkins et al., 2017: 944) was followed by the supervisor identifying the 'problem' and providing a 'solution' with a 'tendency for the advice to concern procedural actions such as completing paperwork or arranging a meeting' (Wilkins et al., 2017: 946). These rapid jumps from a descriptive narrative, to a 'problem', and then to an administrative response to the problem, left little scope for exploring the issues raised by the case in a wider sense. 'Case discussions often included references to risk but it was more common to find risks being "named" than discussed in-depth' (Wilkins et al., 2017: 946):

> For example, whilst the social worker would say if they were worried about substance misuse, we found no discussions that explored how the child

> experienced this, whether the risk related to the parent's behaviour or directly to the substance or both, whether the risk resulted from the parent's use of the substance or from their procurement (e.g. because drug dealers visit the home), or both and so on. (Wilkins et al., 2017: 946)

And there was little discussion of feelings:

> Case discussions also tend not to include emotions, either of the worker or children and families. This is not to say managers were uncaring. In almost all recordings, managers 'check in' at the start, asking how the worker is, how they are coping with their work and so on. However, once the discussion focused on particular families, emotional references were largely absent ... [T]here was only limited consideration of why the social worker felt a particular way or how their feelings might be impacting on their behaviour and decision-making. The most common references were to frustration or other negative affect caused by perceived parental 'resistance'. (Wilkins et al., 2017: 946)

Among the extracts quoted from the transcripts, the following is particularly striking:

> SW: *It was referred by the midwife because of concerns about possible substance misuse, cannabis. I met with mum and started to ask how things were going and she was saying this and that but when he, the dad, when he left, she opened up on me.*
>
> M: *Like what? DV?*
>
> SW: *Not really. When she was younger, she was trafficked here, and pimped and raped and she had another pregnancy, but it didn't make it, and the dad, the new partner, he knows nothing about this. So now, I'm like, what do I do, because I have all this information about mum that dad doesn't know but it will have to go into the assessment so he'll see it.*
>
> M: *You'll have to write two different assessments. Did this happen here or in Ireland?*
>
> SW: *In Ireland I think.*
>
> M: *So, not in our jurisdiction. I'm wondering if mum had a visa when she came here, if she was trafficked?* (Wilkins et al., 2017: 946–7. Italics in original)

So here the social worker has described to the supervisor a really shocking and distressing thing that happened to a woman she is working with – she was trafficked, pimped and raped – and has also told the supervisor how this woman opened up about this when her partner left the room, thus placing considerable trust in the social worker. This, I imagine, would have been a powerful moment for the social worker. But, at least as quoted here, the supervisor's responses are *entirely* administrative: (a) the supervisor says the social worker will have to write two different assessments, (b) the supervisor notes that the crimes against the client happened in another legal jurisdiction, (c) the supervisor asks whether the client had a visa when she was trafficked.

One might wonder *why* the supervisor sidestepped into these bureaucratic questions and away from the obvious emotional charge of this material, but the point I want to make here is that talking about feelings (the client's and the social worker's) really shouldn't be an optional extra in a situation like this because, without considering feelings, it is impossible to think properly about the case at all. Feelings are as central to the job as are (say), the organs of the body or the circulatory system to a surgeon. The reason the social worker was involved in this case, remember, is that a midwife was concerned about the woman's use of cannabis during pregnancy. It is *feelings* that make people choose to use drugs, *feelings* that can make it difficult for a parent to prioritise the needs of a child, *feelings* that make unresponsive parents difficult for children to grow up with. If supervisor and supervisee are to gain some understanding of what is going on for this woman – Why does she use cannabis? What does this tell us about her care of child? What is the likely impact on the child? – they need to consider the likely *emotional* impact of the trafficking and the rape on the way this woman functions. They need to consider how the child may be *feeling* in this situation. They need to consider why the woman doesn't *feel* able to talk about all this in front of her partner but nevertheless *felt* that she wanted to confide it to the social worker. And the supervisor needs to be aware that the social worker's *feelings* will influence the way the social worker tells the story, the aspects the social worker chooses to emphasise, the aspects the social worker may be inclined to play down.

How could the social worker and the supervisor understand the significance of all these feelings without spending a little time on them? The extract from the transcript, in which the discussion jumps straight from this story about trafficking and rape to talk about assessment forms, jurisdictions and visas, reads almost as if the supervisor was trying *not* to understand.

Why people might want to avoid thinking about feelings is something we'll come back to in Chapter 5. (Isabel Menzies Lyth noted how nurses on a busy ward tended to dehumanise their patients in various ways and hide behind administrative procedures as a way of defending themselves against the pain and distress that surrounded them [1988].) But part of the problem (in social work at least) may lie in the fact that the distinction between the 'professional' side of the work and the 'managerial' or administrative side of the work is less clear than it would be in some other contexts. If we take medicine or nursing, for instance, it seems almost too obvious even to need spelling out that administration and management are not substitutes for diagnostic and treatment skills, since they deal with two entirely different realms:

the organisation on the one hand, the human body on the other. Management is vital in healthcare – a hospital with no management would rapidly degenerate into dangerous and unworkable chaos – but no one would suggest that you could have a hospital that ran on management alone, without the need for the clinical judgement and skills of doctors, nurses and other healthcare professionals.

But social workers do not perform surgery or administer drugs and many of their interventions take place through the medium of conversations, meetings and reports, which happen also to be the means through which management is delivered. As a result there is not the same obvious boundary between the professional and the managerial. This makes it easier to shift from professional considerations to talking about purely administrative processes if we find the material distressing, or if we are not confident in our assessment skills or our ability to help people. Nevertheless, a social work organisation whose leaders attended only to the administrative side of things really would be *like a hospital that was only interested in administration, and had no interest in the business of actually treating patients*. (I will leave it to readers from other professions to decide the extent to which this is an issue in their profession also.)

Supervision is one of the ways in which an organisation conveys to staff what is important, and what isn't. If the supervisor shows a keen interest in getting assessment forms signed off on time, but no interest in the assessment process or the quality of the thinking that it contains, then a message is given to staff that thinking is not important, but ticking boxes is.

YOUR EXPERIENCE OF SUPERVISION

People have very varied experiences of supervision. It is worth reflecting on the supervision you have received and asking yourself what it actually consisted of and the degree to which it met professional needs as well as managerial ones.

EXERCISE 1.1

Your supervision history

Make a list of all the supervisors you have had (assuming you've had more than one). Now, for each supervisor write the following:

- Did they take supervision seriously?
- What were they good at?

- What were they not so good at?
- Would you describe their approach to supervision as more managerial and accountability focused or more clinical and focused on professional practice? (Were they more focused on making sure you followed the organisation's requirements, or were they more focused on exploring the issues arising from your casework with you?)
- In later chapters we'll discuss other dimensions of supervision than the 'clinical'/'accountability' aspect we're discussing now. What other aspects are you noticing?
- What were you like as supervisee, and could you, in retrospect, have helped them to provide better supervision?

I include the question 'Did they take supervision seriously?' because that is not always the case. For a supervisor to give the message that she takes supervision seriously, she needs to take time over it, make proper supervision appointments (and stick to them), find a quiet place where supervision can take place uninterrupted, arrive prepared and with a clear agenda, and record sessions well enough to be able to refer back to previous sessions, and build on previous discussions. A supervisor who arrives late for a session, lets herself be interrupted by phone calls, and shows no sign of remembering what was agreed in a previous session, clearly isn't taking supervision seriously and is prioritising some other aspect of her work, or some other aspect of her life, over her supervisory task. (A professional who behaved like that would convey the same message to her clients: 'this meeting isn't very important to me'.)

When I am teaching about supervision, my students tend to report their experience of supervision as being predominantly about accountability – focused on making sure that the organisational framework has been adhered to – rather than clinical, thus confirming the research discussed in the previous section. I have heard quite often about very routinised supervision in which the supervisor seemed almost exclusively focused on ticking boxes in the organisation's administrative system. I have even heard of supervision in which the supervisor is sitting with her back to the supervisee, looking at a screen.

I myself have experienced supervisors who were stronger on the accountability side of things than on the clinical side. However, I have also experienced supervisors who were not very strong on the accountability side either, which can have the effect of leaving the supervisee feeling unboundaried and insecure, like schoolchildren in a class with a teacher who lets them do whatever they want. Accountability supervision may not be sufficient on its own, but it is still very important.

Other dimensions that I notice when I look back on supervision I received include:

- Use of authority. Some supervisors are more controlling than others. Some are more authoritative than others. Being authoritative is of course not the same thing as being controlling (as we'll discuss in Chapter 4), but one aspect of it is a willingness to challenge. I think most supervisors I've had could usefully have been more challenging than they were. I myself could have been more challenging when I was a supervisor.
- Commitment. Some supervisors took supervision more seriously than others. Some were more likely to cancel or to be late, or to allow themselves to be interrupted. Some seem to be giving you the message that they would rather you just got on with it without troubling them with the details of what you are doing.
- Priorities. Supervision serves several purposes. Supervisors vary in what they seem to think is important. Some feel very driven by the need to process cases as quickly as possible (when a supervisor is also the manager of the team, she will always have in the back of her mind the flow of new work that she needs to allocate). Some are more focused on getting it right for the service user. Some make you feel that your own well-being is very important to them.
- Theory. 'Theory' is a knotty issue in social work. Social workers are often not very aware of a formal theory that guides their work, and nor are supervisors, but my supervisors have undoubtedly had different theoretical orientations. One supervisor of mine saw social work as an extension of community work, and placed a strong emphasis on trying to find community solutions. Another was very much into psychoanalysis and tended to interpret things in psychodynamic terms. Some social work organisations, of course, commit themselves to particular theoretical frames. Some are committed to the 'Signs of Safety' model (Signs of Safety, n.d.), which draws on ideas from solution-focused therapy; others sign up to a version of family systems therapy. But supervisors can be interested in theory and in theorising without necessarily being wedded to one particular theoretical model. Supervisors whose approach is strongly managerial tend not to have a strong theoretical orientation in this sense. Indeed, this is one of the weaknesses of a purely 'accountability' approach: it fails to recognise that decisions require not just data but *interpretation* of data, and that interpretation of data necessarily involves having theories.

I do think that I as a *supervisee* could sometimes have done more to help my supervisors. I could have shared more of my feelings and thoughts. I could have talked to them about the kinds of support I needed. To be sure it would be nice if all supervisors delivered exactly what we needed without being asked but supervisors are human, and supervisees need to be willing to be proactive.

EXERCISE 1.2

For supervisors: What kind of supervisor are you?

Are you more of an accountability supervisor or a clinical supervisor?

Almost certainly you are both to some extent, but which side of the job do you find easier? Which side are you more confident with? Which side do you spend the most time on?

Are you strong on keeping all the systems running properly in your team, good at keeping close tabs on recording, a stickler for getting assessments done on time, good at challenging staff who are sloppy about these things? Or do you dislike this side of your job?

Are you good at exploring their work with your supervisees, helping them to get the best possible understanding about what's going on in their clients' worlds? Do you find it interesting noticing your supervisee's biases and blind spots, and, if necessary, challenging these? Are you interested in discussing different ways of looking at a case with your supervisees? Or do you get impatient with this side of the job, and keep it to a minimum?

If you are stronger on the accountability side and less comfortable with the clinical side, why do you think that is?

If you are stronger on the clinical side and less comfortable with the management side, why do you think that is?

If you find yourself to be stronger on the accountability side, you are not unusual. As we have already noted, studies of social work supervision tend to find that supervision errs in this direction. Bourn and Hafford-Letchfield looked at audio-visual recordings of supervision sessions made by managers as part of their submissions for an Advanced/Post Qualifying Award in Social Work. They note:

> Generally evident ... was the sometimes intense interest and concern on the part of the learner managers to meet and prioritise their administrative and managerial responsibilities ... These demands at times conflicted with their supervisees' professional and individual needs for a space that offered the opportunity for reflection and freedom to acknowledge the uncertainty, fear or anxiety that may be present when working with the often complex and worrying situations encountered in social work. (2011: 51–2)

Some suggestions as to possible reasons why supervisors may focus on the accountability side of supervision at the expense of the clinical side are as follows. I don't mean to suggest that all of them apply in every case, or that there aren't other reasons which I haven't thought of.

- They are aware that they are more likely to harm their own reputations by failing to ensure administrative compliance, than by failing to do enough clinical supervision, which is much less easy to measure. (It is easier to measure the completion time for assessments, say, than it is to measure the *quality* of assessments.)
- They are naturally tidy people, who like to keep things clear and distinct and are good at it.
- They are comfortable with the position of being 'the boss'.
- They recognise the importance of keeping the organisational machinery running properly (and perhaps have personal experience of the mess that things get into when that isn't done).
- They respect senior managers, can see what they're trying to achieve and enjoy helping them.
- They are not sure what they can offer on the 'clinical' side of things.
- Sometimes they do not have the same professional background as their supervisees.

In the case of the inexperienced supervisor who doubts that she has enough to offer on the 'clinical' side, I would gently suggest that it may be less difficult than it appears. Just as a new professional practitioner must learn to shut up and listen to clients, resisting the temptation to come up with solutions all the time, so the skill of clinical supervision begins with allowing yourself to listen to others and to live for a while with uncertainty. You don't need to come up with all the answers, or to be wiser than your supervisee. You just need to provide a space within which your supervisee can develop her own thoughts.

A lot of supervisors are stronger on accountability, but it is perfectly possible for a supervisor to err in the opposite direction and be strong on the clinical side and weaker on the accountability side. Here are some reasons why I think some people might be more comfortable with the clinical side of supervision. Again, I don't suggest that all (or any) of these necessarily apply, or that there aren't other reasons.

- They aren't comfortable with being 'the boss' and prefer a role which allows them to feel more like a colleague (in some cases because their supervisees are indeed their former colleagues and perhaps even their friends).
- They are committed to bringing about change for service users and are impatient with management systems which sometimes feel like they are irrelevant to client needs.

- They are aware that clinical supervision is often under-emphasised and want to rectify that (or are aware that clinical expertise in general is often undervalued and wish to rectify this).
- They find managerial tasks boring and prefer to avoid them where possible.
- They enjoy the challenge of exploring the client world and thinking imaginatively about interventions.
- They want to be liked and admired by practitioners.

So there are many reasons both for being too exclusively 'accountability' or too exclusively 'clinical' in your approach to supervision. The key point is that, if your job requires you to do both types of supervision, you do need to do both, even if this means challenging yourself in a way that feels uncomfortable.

ACCOUNTABILITY SUPERVISION AND CLINICAL SUPERVISION COMBINED

In theory the two kinds of supervision can come from different people, and sometimes this happens in practice. But more usually, practitioners have a single supervisor who has the same professional training as themselves and who (one hopes), takes on both the accountability and clinical aspects of supervision. This is not to say that other supervision arrangements do not also exist in the human service context. For instance, social workers, youth workers etc. may supplement the supervision they receive from their line manager with peer supervision of one kind or another (akin to 'clinical supervision' as outlined above). This may include group supervision, in which most of the input is provided by peers and colleagues, rather than managers. And sometimes supervision is split, with a line manager providing a predominantly accountability type of supervision, and a senior practitioner providing something closer to clinical supervision.

However, generally speaking, the person a human service worker answers to in accountability terms, is also supposed to be their primary source of clinical supervision. In plain words, the person who is checking up on you to make sure you do your job according to the requirements of the organisation, is also the person to whom you are expected to turn to help you discuss your worries and doubts and help you figure out what is going on.

This is true of the supervisors of qualified staff, but it is equally true of practice educators who supervise students. Practice educators (of course) are expected to support and encourage students and help them to grow in skills, knowledge and confidence, but are also required to ensure that the student's practice is safe and appropriate and decide whether the student should pass or fail the placement, and these are *accountability* roles in the terms I am using, even though the practice educator, in all probability, is not a manager.

There are drawbacks to combining clinical and accountability supervision because sometimes they pull the supervisee in different ways. A supervisee, whether a qualified professional or a student, needs to be able to share her feelings openly in order to get the best out of clinical supervision, but may be reluctant to admit to doubts or lack of confidence (or indeed mistakes) to a manager who might question her suitability for the job, or a practice educator who could decide not to give her a pass mark for the placement. The supervisee's position in relation to the supervisor here is analogous to that of an involuntary client (for example a parent whose child has been taken into care) in relation to her social worker. The parent needs to be honest about the difficulties she's having with her child in order to get the most out of the help available, but may be reluctant to be completely honest for fear of coming over as unable to cope: a good social worker needs to be sensitive to this dilemma, and find ways of helping the parents negotiate it, and the same is true of the supervisor in relation to the supervisee or student. (There will be more on this in Chapter 5.) 'Simone', a social worker who is quoted in a study by Richard Ingram, says: 'I suspect that being emotional is seen as not functioning and would become an occupational health issue – my supervision is not a place to share emotions, it is a task focussed exercise telling me what to do and when to do it' (2015: 908).

So, yes, there are tensions between the two kinds of supervision which can make combining them difficult. But splitting them into separate roles carried out by different people also has drawbacks. These include the possibility of the supervisee being given a different message as to what to do by two different supervisors, or of the supervisee being able to confide information to one which is withheld from the other. In fact I find it hard to imagine a system in which there was an *absolute* split between clinical and accountability supervision. It seems to me that the 'clinical' supervisor in such a division of labour must have at least *some* accountability responsibilities, even if only a responsibility to pass information on to the manager who is primarily accountable for the supervisee's practice.

And, though combining clinical and accountability supervision may present some challenges, it is simply an example of the bringing together of authority and support roles that is very common in many areas of life. Parents do this, teachers do it, and social workers, youth workers and many other professionals do it in their work with service users. (I will come back to this in Chapter 4 when discussing the use of authority.) So there is nothing particularly unusual about combining accountability supervision with clinical supervision. Fears that talking honestly about feelings in supervision will be seen as not coping are understandable, but a good supervisor should be able to alleviate these fears by discussing the issue with the supervisee (or student), and being explicit that powerful feelings are normal and appropriate, and can be helpful to understanding the world of a service user.

MANAGEMENT VERSUS SUPERVISION

I've discussed the tension between accountability supervision and clinical supervision so far in this chapter, but it's important to remember too that few people are *just* supervisors. Staff supervision is typically just one part of the supervisor's job. In social work, supervisors (other than practice teachers) tend to be managers or senior practitioners with a number of other responsibilities. So, in addition to the accountability/clinical tension within supervision, there can be tensions between the management role in general and the supervisory role. One instance of this (which I'll discuss further in Chapter 7) arises from the fact that the manager of a team is responsible for getting work done, and may be very aware of a backlog of work that needs allocating. This can be a considerable source of anxiety. In a supervision session, a manager who is worried about work that needs allocating may be predisposed to hear that a current case is no longer a priority and can be closed, and may find it harder to hear or notice signs that this current case still in fact needs a lot of work. This is an example of the kind of pressures that can affect what we notice or fail to notice which I will discuss in more detail in Chapters 5. One of the functions of supervision is to try and correct for the ways in which the supervisee's perceptions may be affected by such pressures. But of course supervisors are also human and not immune from the pressures of their own.

CONCLUDING NOTES FOR SUPERVISORS AND SUPERVISEES

Notes for supervisors (including practice educators)

I have drawn a distinction in this chapter between accountability aspects of supervision and clinical aspects of supervision. Supervisors vary along a spectrum, with some being much more comfortable with the accountability side of things, some with the clinical side.

If you have recently moved into a management position, for instance, and are supervising people who used to be your colleagues you may find it difficult to check up on your supervisees' work, and challenge them about things like tardy recording, or punctuality, and you may find it easy to offer clinical supervision as one professional

(Continued)

to another. You may then end up being stronger on the 'clinical' side of supervision and not so good on the 'accountability side': something to be careful about, because important things in the team may begin to slip.

If, on the other hand, you find it easier to concentrate on the more clear-cut nature of accountability supervision – procedures, time-scales and so forth – you may end up being stronger on the accountability side. This is *also* something to be careful about, because, though your staff may be doing their recording on time, the quality of their work may begin to slip.

Your personality is relevant here too (see Chapter 4). The accountability side can be hard for people who have a strong need to please others, and hate confrontation. The clinical side can be hard for perfectionists who feel uncomfortable if they are not in charge of everything.

However, if you are able to recognise where you sit on that spectrum and why, you are in a good position to identify what you need to work on (perhaps with help from your own supervisor, if you are lucky). This doesn't mean that you have to be like every other supervisor, because there are many different ways of doing accountability supervision and many different ways of doing clinical supervision, and you need to find the ways that suit your personality.

But mastering the art of combining the accountability and clinical aspects of supervision is important, not just for the reasons already discussed in this chapter but because most human service workers are themselves performing roles that involve balancing the use of authority with offering support. You need to be able to model this.

Notes for supervisees (including students on placement)

If you are a student or a newly qualified practitioner, there is no reason you should know what you ought to expect from supervision. The point of this chapter has been to draw your attention to the fact that supervisors are, or should be, balancing two rather different kinds of function, and you should expect both kinds of supervision. Interestingly, this mirrors a balance that you yourself need to be trying to achieve in your own work and which you may well be finding difficult, balancing your role as the representative of an organisation, and sometimes even of the state, with your role as a helper and supporter. (In relation to your own work, you could ask yourself the same question that I asked above of supervisors: which aspect comes more naturally to you and why?)

If your supervision is not giving you what you need, then you need to think of ways of addressing this. As I suggested above, it is possible to ask for something more, though of course this can be difficult when your supervisor is in a more powerful position than you are. But it may also be that part of the problem is you. If you do not share with your supervisor what is really going on for you, then your supervisor will have less to work on than if you do. This is not to say that you should be constantly telling your supervisor when you feel a bit anxious: feeling a bit anxious does, I am afraid, come with the territory. But you should discuss with your supervisor aspects of the job that you notice you are finding particularly difficult. You should also be willing to do some thinking yourself and then present your thinking to your supervisor. If you simply ask your supervisor to tell you what to do, you are basically asking your supervisor to do your thinking for you, which isn't conducive to learning, and doesn't help the supervisor to give you good clinical supervision.

Sometimes you may have a supervisor who simply isn't able to offer what you need. In rare cases this may be such a problem for you that you need to take it up with someone else (if you are a student, you could take it up with your college tutor). Often it is possible to find a work around by finding an informal source of supplementary clinical supervision in the form of a colleague you can talk things over with.

CHAPTER SUMMARY

This chapter has explored a fundamental dichotomy between two kinds of supervision, both of which are necessary in human service organisations. In the next chapter we will look at other ways of dividing up supervision, including different functions, different interests served, and different stages in the supervisory context, but also different contexts and methods.

2

COMPONENTS OF SUPERVISION

CONTENTS

In the previous chapter I divided supervision into accountability supervision and clinical supervision. In this chapter, drawing on the work of other writers on supervision, I'm going to break supervision down into much smaller parts. I'll look at these components of supervision under three headings which come straight from the '4 × 4 × 4' model developed by Tony Morrison and Jane Wonnacott: *functions, stakeholders* and *elements* (Wonnacott, 2012). '*Functions*' refers to the purposes that supervision serves. '*Stakeholders*' refers to the various different interest groups and agendas who may be affected by the kind of supervision that is offered (most obviously, service users and supervisees, but there are others). '*Elements*' refers to the supervisory process: the different aspects that are, or should be, explored when a topic is discussed in supervision.

'FUNCTIONS' OF SUPERVISION

Alfred Kadushin (1976; most recent edition is Kadushin and Harkness, 2014) suggested that supervision could be divided into *management, support* and *education* (or *development* as the latter is also called), a three-way split which has been picked up by several writers. Hughes and Pengelly (1997: 42) offer their own version of it as: (1) '*Managing service delivery*', (2) '*Facilitating practitioners' professional development*' and (3) '*Focusing on practitioners' work*'.

Richards et al. (1990) added a fourth function to Kadushin's. In addition to *Management, Support* and *Development*, they proposed *Mediation* between the supervisee and the organisation. And, in their 4 × 4 × 4 model, Morrison (2005) and Wonnacott (2012) adopt these same four 'functions' which Morrison summarises as follow in terms of 'objectives':

1 Competent, accountable performance (management or normative function) *[Management]*
2 Continuing professional development (developmental/formative function) *[Development]*
3 Personal support (supportive/restorative function) *[Support]*
4 Engaging the individual with the organisation (mediation function) *[Mediation]*

(Morrison, 2005: 32. The terms in italics are the ones used by Wonnacott, 2012, in her exposition of the 4 × 4 × 4 model and I've added them here for clarity.)

About mediation

'Mediation' refers to the responsibility of the supervisor to communicate the needs and requirements of the organisation to the supervisee in a way that the supervisee can apply to her practice, while also communicating the needs and perspectives of the supervisee to the centre of the organisation. This task of facilitating two-way communication is something that goes on not just in supervision sessions but in other forums such as team meetings, and is a particularly characteristic part of the role of managers of front-line staff in any organisation. David Sims (2003) describes the difficult role of middle managers (which in this context at least can mean any manager between the top and bottom of a hierarchy) in terms of 'story-telling'. 'Middle managers,' Sims writes, '... are expected to weave a narrative for those who work under them to believe in, and to be able to give a coherent narrative account of their performance to their superiors' (Sims, 2003: 1196). In the specific context of a supervision session, this mediation role can often mean trying to explain to supervisees why an action they want to take is not possible within the organisation (perhaps for budgetary reasons), or why they must prioritise an action, such as completing forms, which is important to the organisation but does not seem to the supervisee to directly benefit service users. This can be a difficult and rather thankless task.

But part of mediation, as Jane Wonnacott puts it, is to 'use policies and procedures as a framework for good practice, encouraging flexibility and innovation in the interests of service users' or even sometimes to 'provide an appropriate "buffer" to organisational demands and assist the social worker in maintaining a focus on good practice' (2012: 32–3). In other words, part of mediation may be for the supervisor to take organisational demands on her own shoulders to some extent and protect good practice from overly rigid application of organisational requirements.

I will have more to say about mediation in Chapter 8.

Clarification: a fifth function?

I think a fifth function ought to be added to the list, which I will call *clarification*. This relates particularly to the 'clinical' side of supervision, and you will see what I mean by it, if you consider the case discussed in Chapter 1 of a therapist who pays a colleague to provide her with supervision. I suggested there, that the main benefit of this is that the supervisor's greater detachment means that she sees things from a different perspective and will notice things that the therapist herself misses because of her personal involvement with the case. The supervisor doesn't know more about the case than the therapist – in fact she knows less – but by asking questions from her different perspective, the supervisor helps the therapist to disentangle her thoughts and impressions, and thus see more clearly.

The Wonnacott model gives a lot of attention to what I am calling clarification, but includes it as part of the support function. It seems to me, though, that what is involved in clarification is not simply support, but a collaborative process whose purpose is to *refine the understanding* of both supervisee and supervisor so as to deliver the best possible service. It is distinct from 'support' in the sense of looking after staff (what Proctor [1988] called the *'restorative'* function, something I will come back to in Chapter 8), because it is not about the organisation's duty of care to its workers, but is about adding value to the work they do. I therefore wonder if clarification deserves to be seen as a function in its own right? If so, we have five functions, illustrated in Table 2.1.

Table 2.1 Five functions of supervision

Management	Ensuring that the agency's responsibilities are being met in a way that meets the agency's standards and requirements.
Development	Helping staff to learn and to grow in skills and knowledge.
Restorative (personal support)	Helping staff to deal with the demands and pressures of the job.
Mediation	Interpreting the agency's needs to staff members, and vice versa.
Clarification (casework support)	Refinement of practice by providing a safe space and an alternative perspective to help develop ideas.

(Ultimately of course, the word used doesn't matter, and different systems of classification are often equally valid. The important thing is that this work takes place.)

In the previous chapter I made a simple (and somewhat simplistic) two-way distinction between 'accountability supervision', such as you find in any organisation, and 'clinical supervision' which is necessary in human services. Of the five functions, 'management' is clearly on the 'accountability' side, and 'clarification' (where the supervisor draws directly on her own professional skills) is definitely on the 'clinical' side. 'Mediation' is on the 'accountability' side, since it is a management function in any well-run organisation. 'Support' and 'development' on the other hand, are arguably both 'accountability' and 'clinical' functions (see Figure 2.1).

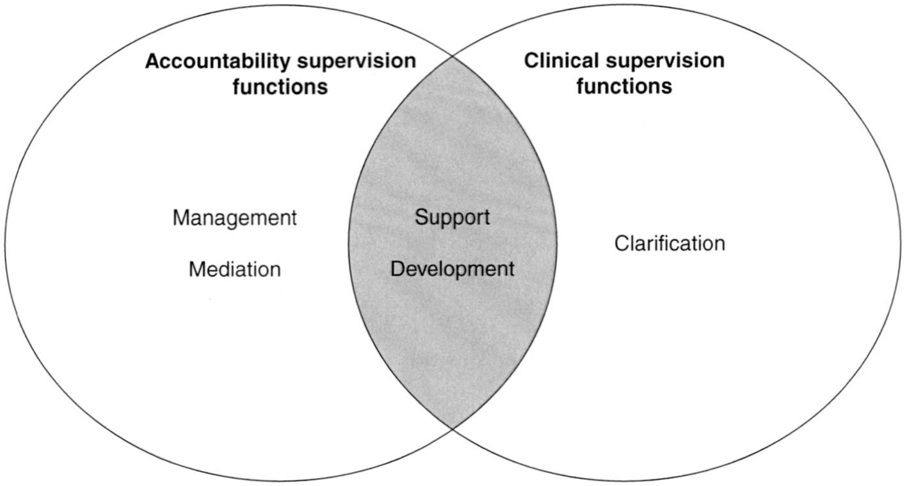

Figure 2.1 Accountability and clinical functions

'STAKEHOLDERS'/INTERESTS/AGENDAS

There are a number of different groups and agendas which may be affected by what goes on in supervision in the sense that, if a supervisor places a strong emphasis on a particular agenda, or the needs of a particular group, then that agenda or group is likely to benefit, while if a supervisor shows no interest in a particular agenda, and does not seem concerned about the interests of a particular group, then that agenda or group will lose out. The 4 × 4 × 4 model offers four *stakeholders*:

- Service users
- Staff
- The organisation
- Partners (that is, other agencies with which the organisation collaborates) (Wonnacott, 2012: 53)

In the course of my teaching, two other important stakeholders, quite distinct from any of the four above, have been pointed out to me by thoughtful students:

- The community. (In youth justice work, for instance, the community is supposed to be a beneficiary of the service, and there are many other areas of work in which the community at large has a direct interest in the work carried out by the agency: for instance, the community is likely to be interested in the management of a children's home in its area.)
- The profession. (Supervision plays an important role in developing a profession, maintaining its standards and so protecting its identity and reputation.)

Morrison and Wonnacott's four stakeholder groups can also be broken down further. For instance, 'service users' are not really a monolithic group and do not necessarily all have the same interests as one another, and so are arguably not a single set of stakeholders. I find it helpful to divide service users into *primary* service users and *secondary* service users. In the case of family social work or teaching the primary service users are children, the secondary service users are parents or other carers, while in work with older people the primary service users are the older people themselves, the secondary service users are their spouses, daughters, sons or whoever else is involved in providing informal care. We know the needs of primary and secondary service users are not necessarily the same and may sometimes pull in opposite directions, and we also know the needs of secondary users are important and must be addressed if they are to continue to support primary service users. One of the tasks of a supervisor may be to help the social worker juggle these different and competing needs. As I'll discuss in Chapter 5, individual professionals differ in who they find it easiest to identify with. Depending on their own history and their circumstances, some identify most readily with primary service users, others identify most easily with parents or carers. Supervision may play an important role in helping to maintain a balanced approach.

The same is true of the category 'staff': it includes a range of stakeholders whose interests may be different to one another's. Hopefully, the supervisee is a beneficiary of supervision. (Hawkins and Smith [2006] include a specific 'resourcing function' of supervision which is to do with helping staff to recover from the emotional impact of their work.) But the supervisor is also, one hopes, a beneficiary, and so are other staff members when supervision addresses a worker's relationship with her colleagues.

Similarly, while the 'organisation' is certainly a stakeholder in supervision, it isn't a single monolithic interest either, but rather a set of competing and sometimes contradictory interests, reflecting the various needs of the people who make it up. Often a supervisor will feel pressure from more senior members of the organisation to focus on specific issues, particularly if the organisation itself is being put under pressure from outside: these might be speeding up assessments, reducing costs, freeing up hospital beds, reducing (or sometimes increasing) the number of children subject to child protection plans, and countless other targets and goals. Managers at every level of the organisation have reputations to consider, and the reputation of the whole organisation is important for most people who work in it: this can result in pressure not to take risks, or a preoccupation with 'back-covering' which again can play out in the supervisory process, though the organisation also has an interest in delivering high quality casework, supporting the development of staff and retaining high quality staff.

So, if we are looking at who or what has a stake in supervision, we could easily generate quite a long list of different *interests* or *agendas* which the supervisory process could serve (or could fail to serve), and which themselves can both support and contradict one another. Here are just a few:

- Optimising outcomes for service users (though of course good outcomes may be defined in many different ways!)
- Keeping within budget
- Maintaining staff morale and retaining staff
- Allowing the supervisor an accurate picture of what is going on in the team
- Improving relations between different parts of the organisation, or between the organisation and partner agencies (for example, supervision might address how a social worker is to deal constructively with another professional from another agency who the social worker is experiencing as uncooperative or difficult)
- Achieving specific goals or targets (for instance: freeing up hospital beds)
- Avoiding tragic outcomes for service users
- Minimising reputational risk to the organisation and to senior managers
- Building skills and expertise

- Maintaining cohesion within a team (for example by addressing the problem of a team member seen by colleagues as not pulling her weight).

The key point here is the supervisor has to strike a balance between these different interests.

EXERCISE 2.1

Balancing different beneficiaries and interests

I have just made a list of various interests/beneficiaries served by supervision. It's not exhaustive. Try and make a similar list for yourself of the various different interests that you are aware of, and which you may well experience as different and competing pressures.

Try and distinguish between what you experience as direct pressures on you yourself, and what seem to you to be pressures on your partner in the supervision process (i.e. if you are a supervisor, your partner would be the supervisee, but if you are looking at this from the point of view of a supervisee, then your partner is the supervisor). Supervisees tend to feel more direct pressure on them from service users or carers, who they know personally and must face with the decisions made in the meeting, but supervisors are typically more aware of unallocated work, and of the concerns of more senior managers.

But notice too that not all the pressures on you in the supervisory context come from outside. Some come from within yourself.

Now, having compiled your list, pick some items from the list and ask yourself the following questions:

- What would be the consequences if supervision focused too much on this at the expense of all the others?
- What would be the consequences if supervision ignored this?

Finally, looking at the whole list, ask yourself:

- Which of these do I like addressing and come back to as often as I can?
- Which of these do I dislike addressing, and avoid as much as possible?
- What other, more personal, factors are in play that influence my preferences as to what I like to focus on? (This could include, for instance, your own need to be liked, or to be seen as tough, or to be in control, or your lack of confidence in some areas and confidence in others.)

Probably you will agree that it would be a mistake to focus too much on any one item on your list at the expense of the others. For instance it is good to use supervision to check up on the well-being of the supervisee, but supervision that focused too much on the needs of the supervisee (which can happen if the supervisor starts to think of the supervisee more as a client) would be indulgent and even dangerous, because it has shifted its attention away from the main purpose of the agency. Similarly, while it is (of course) good to focus on improving outcomes for service users and the community, since this is (or should be) what the agency exists to do, that doesn't mean that organisational or staff needs can simply be ignored. The long-term viability of the organisation and its ability to deliver services depends on its being able to maintain its reputation, and retain its staff.

I imagine that all supervisors have some preferences as to what they like to focus on. We tend to prefer to do tasks we know we are good at, or are most likely to be thanked for. But obviously these preferences need to be kept in check. In the same way, practitioners probably always have preferences as to which service users they find rewarding to work with, but one of the tasks of supervision is to ensure that these preferences are likewise kept in check and do not prevent practitioners from prioritising their work on the basis of need.

It is useful to think about the various interests that are served by supervision, because it then becomes more visible to us if our style of supervision is overly skewed, like the practice of a worker who spends too much time with her favourite service user and avoids the one who makes her feel uncomfortable.

EXERCISE 2.2

Consequences of imbalance

What would be the consequences for practice if a supervisor focused too much on one or other of the following interests at the expense of the others?

- Supervisee's well-being
- Organisation's need to avoid reputational harm
- Supervisor's need to allocate new work
- The service user under discussion

My suggestions are:

- Supervision that focuses too exclusively on the supervisee's well-being is likely to turn into a kind of counselling session with the supervisor as counsellor. The well-being of supervisees is important but it is not the purpose of the agency.

- Supervision that focuses too much on the organisation's need to avoid reputational harm, will tend to be very risk-averse, and very much focused on ensuring that the supervisee creates a visible record of the fact that her decisions and actions have all been discussed and agreed with other agencies. Minimising risk, accurate recording and good inter-agency communication are all very important things, but they are supposed to be means to an end. If the supervisee is encouraged always to choose the option that is safest in reputational terms, this may result in overly defensive practice which is not in the best interests of the service user.
- If the supervisor has work that she badly needs to allocate, she may pressure the supervisee to close cases, and may be tempted to minimise, or even discount altogether, concerns the supervisee has about existing work. This could become dangerous if the supervisor's anxiety about unallocated work is so great that she becomes unable to hear how much work the supervisee still needs to do to make her existing cases safe.
- It seems at first sight strange to suggest that there could be too much focus on the needs of a service user, but every service user is, in effect, competing against other current and potential service users for the services of the agency, and too much emphasis on one can lead to others losing out.

'ELEMENTS' OR 'STAGES' OF SUPERVISION: THE SUPERVISION CYCLE

Having looked at the functions of supervision and the various stakeholders/beneficiaries/interests it serves, we can now turn to the process of supervision itself and ask what it consists of and what stages it moves through. We are now discussing, not just what, or who, supervision is for, but what it *is*, and I will focus in particular on the function that I have called *clarification*. Again, there are several ways of looking at this. Davys and Beddoe (2010) suggest that, after preparation and agenda setting, a supervision session should move through a cycle of four parts that they call Event, Exploration, Experimentation, and Evaluation. Hawkins and Shohet (2012) propose what they call the CLEAR supervision model which includes five stages: Contract, Listen, Explore, Action, Review. Wonnacott (2012) offers four 'elements' (the final '4' in the 4 × 4 × 4 model): Experience, Reflection, Analysis, and Action Planning. Although there are many overlaps between these models, I will adopt Wonnacott's supervisory cycle (which itself is based on Kolb's 'Learning Cycle' [1984]) as my framework here because I have found it the most useful, partly because of the particular attention it pays to the emotional response or gut feeling of the supervisee, as something that precedes analysis, and partly because of the powerful idea of blocked cycles and cycles with missing stages which Morrison (2005) and Wonnacott (2012) have developed as part of their model.

Morrison (2005) and Wonnacott's (2012) four elements – Experience, Reflection, Analysis and Action Planning – are listed below with my own commentary (their equivalents in the Kolb cycle are: Concrete Experience, Reflective Observation, Abstract Conceptualisation and Active Experimentation). They constitute the different processes through which the supervision process should move as supervisor and supervisee address a particular agenda item (meaning that the same processes will be gone through separately for all the substantive items on the agenda). It is important to note that these authors use these words, and in particular the words Experience and Reflection, in a much more restricted sense than we would use them in everyday speech and I capitalise them here to emphasise that they are being used as names, rather than in their more general ordinary sense.

1 *Experience* – By this is meant, roughly, 'what has happened'. For example if the agenda item is the case of 'Mrs Smith', there have perhaps been a home visit, a phone call with a doctor, and a letter from a housing officer since the last supervision. The content of the visit, the phone call and the letter are what is meant by 'Experience'. But it is important to remember that what is actually brought to the supervision session is not the Experience as such, but the supervisee's summary of that Experience, based on what she noticed, what she remembers and/or recorded of what she noticed, and what, out of the things she remembers, she considers salient to the discussion. One of the tasks of the supervisor when exploring Experience is to ensure that important details are not being overlooked. I will discuss this further in Chapter 5.

The next two stages of supervision are aimed at helping the supervisee interpret this Experience and come to usable conclusions:

2 *Reflection* – In the Wonnacott/Morrison model, Reflection refers to considering the supervisee's feelings about the Experience. (So for instance, in a case study about a client called Sara whose flat had been damaged by fire, Wonnacott suggests that the following are useful questions for the Reflection stage: 'What were your immediate feelings when Sara told you about the fire?' 'Does Sara remind you of anybody?' and 'What feelings are you left with?' [2012: 59].) I am going to discuss Reflection in this sense in Chapter 5, but I will note very briefly here that feelings are in fact the quickest and most instinctive way in which we make sense of a situation. (If I see a man coming at me with a knife, I feel fear, and an urgent need to run or protect myself, well before I have time to ask myself in a more thought-out way what might be going on.) For this reason it would be foolish to ignore them. But we have to be cautious about feelings because they are subjective

and linked very much to our own personal life history. (Hence the question, 'Does Sara remind you of anybody?') It is certainly not unprofessional to think about feelings – far from it – but it is unprofessional to ACT on feelings without giving thought to where they come from and what they mean.

We should note at this point that, although these four elements are presented here as successive stages in a cycle, in reality it will often be necessary to go back and forth. For example if the supervisee seems to have powerful feelings about some aspect of the case, it may be necessary to encourage her to go back to Experience to try and remember more detail, by asking questions such as, 'What exactly was going on when you started to feel so uneasy?' or 'What exactly did Mrs Patel say or do in the meeting to make you come away feeling so much more concerned about her attitude than you were before?'

3 *Analysis* – A horse bolts in fear when it sees something unfamiliar. From a safe distance it stops and tries to work out what is going on. Feelings may be the first rapid initial stage of interpretation in response to new events, but they should not be the last. It is only in the most extreme emergencies that we need to act on feelings alone. Almost always there is time to think about the feelings, weigh them up, consider the extent to which they are linked to the Experience being discussed, and the extent to which they may be linked to aspects of the supervisee's experience that are irrelevant to the present context. Having done that preliminary work in the Reflection stage, we now move to the Analysis stage which is about forming a kind of provisional picture of what is going on in the world of the service user. This typically involves coming to a judgement about risks and strengths in the situation, and about the relationships between the various people involved. If the case has been discussed before, this part of the process might also involve revisiting previous hypotheses and re-evaluating them in the light of what has since happened. (I discuss the Analysis stage more fully in Chapter 6.)

Again, it may be that, as this stage progresses, it is necessary to go back to Experience or to Reflection. ('We have formed this hypothesis, but do the facts as we know them really support it?' 'We have come to this judgement but do your guts say it's right, and, if not, why not?')

4 *Action Planning* – Having come to some sort of hypothesis about what is happening, the next stage is to plan an action. That action could be to close the case, or to gather more information, or it could be to offer a service or make an intervention of some kind. The outcome of these actions then becomes another body of Experience to explore in a future supervision and the cycle comes round again (see Chapter 6).

The whole cycle (and my take on it) is summarised in Figure 2.2.

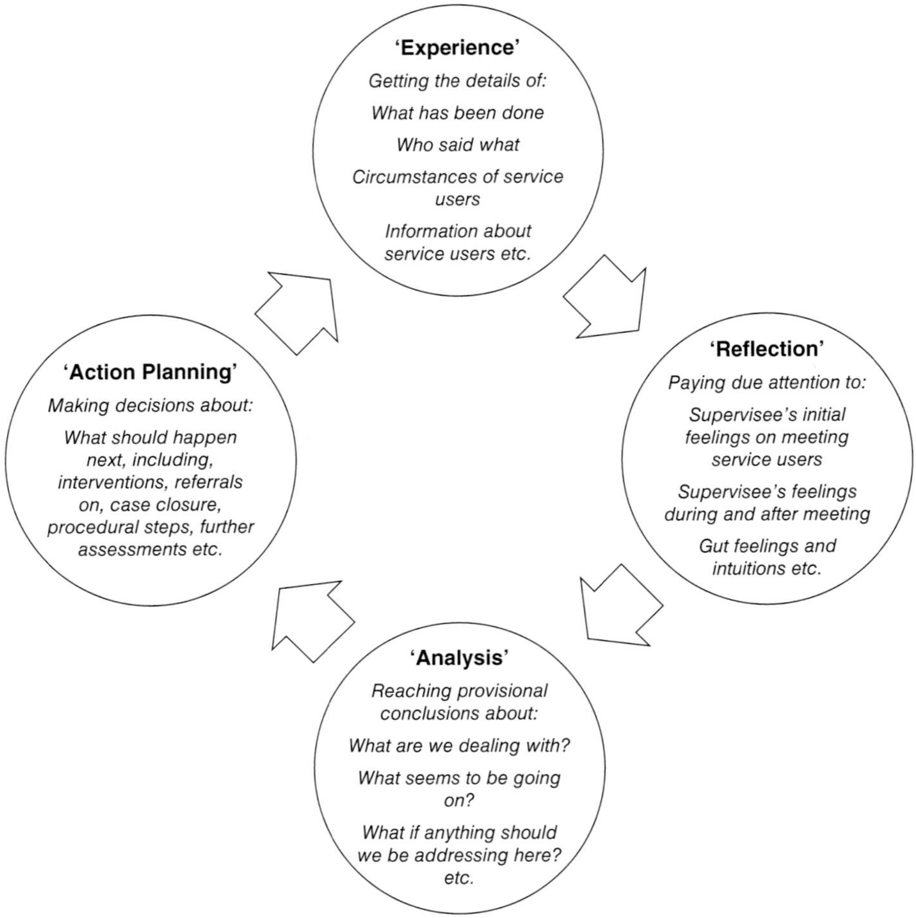

Figure 2.2 The supervision cycle (after Wonnacott, 2012, with my own comments in italics, reproduced by permission of Jessica Kingsley Publishers Limited)

SHORT-CIRCUITING THE CYCLE

An important insight of the Morrison/Wonnacott model is that the cycle can easily be short-circuited, as happens when people try to jump straight from Experience to Action without Reflection or Analysis. Sometimes supervisee and supervisor do this together, agreeing an action plan of action on only a very superficial understanding of what is going on. (The reasoning might go something like: 'This is clearly an X case. What we always do in X cases is Y. Therefore we should do Y.')

It can also happen that a supervisee narrates her Experience and the supervisor then simply tells her what to do. In Chapter 1, I discussed a study by Wilkins et al. (2017) which found that this was actually the normal pattern in the supervision sessions they recorded. This approach can be tempting for the supervisor if she is short of time (and it can meet other needs for the supervisor too: having staff rely on her for every decision may help her feel important and useful). Some supervisees, too, particularly if they are inexperienced or unconfident, may positively welcome the chance to hand over the decision-making to the supervisor and so free themselves from the anxiety of possibly making the wrong decision. So this short-circuiting pattern can be mutually reinforcing, just as a similar pattern between service users and practitioners (the service user presents a problem and the practitioner offers a solution) can also be mutually reinforcing.

But, while short-circuiting the cycle in this way may sometimes be necessary when time is limited, it is not a good idea in general. This is because, firstly, it means that decisions about actions are taken on a very superficial basis, and by the person with less detailed knowledge of the case. And secondly, it deprives the supervisee of an opportunity to develop the skills of reflection and analysis, undermining the Developmental function of supervision, rather as if a mathematics teacher were to write a problem on the board and then tell her students the answer, without giving them the opportunity of trying to work it out for themselves.

THE 'BLOCKED CYCLE'

The concept of the blocked cycle (Morrison, 2005) seems to me to have very considerable explanatory power. Briefly, the idea is that supervisees may get stuck at one of the four stages of the supervisory cycle and find it difficult to move on. (Supervisors can also get stuck in the same way, of course, and supervisors and supervisees can even collude together in being stuck, but supervisors are less likely to be blocked because they are in a position of relative detachment in relation to the case material.) Before continuing it might be worth thinking for yourself what it might mean for a supervisee to be stuck in one or other part of the cycle:

EXERCISE 2.3

Where supervisees get blocked

What might it look like if a supervisee became stuck at one of the four stages (Experience, Reflection, Analysis, Action Planning)? Jot down a few thoughts for each.

Is any of these familiar to you from your own experience as a supervisor or supervisee?

Why do you think people get stuck at this particular stage?

Morrison's proposal is that these blockages are an attempt by the supervisee to manage anxiety. The way I would put it is that people get stuck at one or other part of the cycle because they are, for whatever reason, afraid to move on, or back, to one or more of the other parts.

Stuck in Experience

Supervisees who are stuck on Experience spend a lot of time describing the situation in great detail, perhaps including details that are irrelevant or trivial. You may recall that the study by Wilkins et al. (2017), discussed in the previous chapter, referred to the tendency of social workers in supervision to produce a 'verbal deluge' of information about the case under discussion. I remember a social worker telling me admiringly about the colour the radiators were painted in the house that she visited, and the colour scheme of the paintwork on the stairs. Someone stuck on Experience will resist efforts to get them to talk about their feelings, or to offer any thoughts about what might be going on because they do not want to Reflect on their feelings, or come to conclusions through Analysis which might be uncomfortable. Often supervisees who do this may be hoping or expecting that the supervisor will short-circuit the interpretation stages for them and simply tell them what to do. (And many supervisors are only too happy to oblige, as the Wilkins et al. study illustrates.) But supervisees who are very stuck in Experience may be resistant even to receiving instructions because they are afraid of the Action Plan that they might be asked to implement.

Looking back, I recall that the social worker who expressed such fascination with the interior décor had been visiting a client who was extremely aggressive and intimidating, had served time in prison for a violent offence and was now looking after a child who was a relative of his. The purpose of her visit was to begin an assessment of his suitability for this role. I imagine she didn't particularly want to notice things that might call his suitability into question because, if we had concluded that the man was not a suitable carer for the child it would mean confronting him, which was probably quite a daunting prospect.

Stuck in Reflection

Supervisees who are stuck in Reflection (in the particular sense that the word is used in this model) will talk a great deal about their feelings, whether positive or negative, but be reluctant to move on to Analysis or Action Planning, or back to Experience. Outside of the work context, I have sometimes met people who have behaved like this in respect of their personal lives: people who are constantly telling their friends how desperately unhappy they are in their marriages, for instance, but who never seem to do anything about it. (The cycle, and the possibility of its being blocked, are ideas that are relevant not only to supervision but to decision-making in general.) In such situations it is presumably the fear of coming to a conclusion which they would rather not reach that prevents people from moving on from endlessly rehearsing feelings. People in this position may seem to be hoping that someone else will tell them what is going on and what to do about it, yet if any kind of Analysis or Action is proposed to them, they immediately find reasons to oppose it. (Overcoming this very human reluctance to move on from feelings to coming to a decision and acting on it, is the entire basis of the counselling technique known as Motivational Interviewing [Miller and Rollnick, 2012]). Jane Wonnacott observes that 'the supervisee who responds to anxiety by seeking reassurance from others may find it hard to move on from the "reflection stage"' (2012: 162).

Stuck in Analysis

Supervisees who are stuck in Analysis are willing to theorise at length about what might be going on, and may be drawn to psychological theory the better to do it, but are reluctant to move forward into any kind of Action. One way of getting stuck in Analysis is to engage in an endless cycle of assessments, each one of which is supposed to add additional information to the overall picture. People can get stuck in Analysis when they have skipped over Reflection because there are feelings they are reluctant to examine. However, it seems to me that the main reason for being stuck in Analysis is probably the fear of acting and getting it wrong. Social work and similar human service professions operate, as I discussed in the previous chapter, in Schön's 'swampy lowlands' where judgements must be made but absolutely definite answers cannot be found, and in my experience people who are stuck in Analysis sometimes seem to have persuaded themselves that if only they gather enough data and think long enough and hard enough, they will finally know without a shadow of doubt what is the right thing to do, and free themselves from the fear of making the wrong call. And yet absolute certainty is never really going to happen.

As with 'stuck in Reflection', we can see people being stuck in Analysis in a non-work context as well as in supervision. And being stuck in Analysis is also something that happens at the institutional level. Isabel Menzies Lyth observed of the nurses in her famous study that 'all decisions are ... necessarily attended by some uncertainty as to their outcome and consequently by some conflict and anxiety' (1960: 104), and that this anxiety was addressed, among other ways, by 'a common practice of checking and rechecking decisions for validity and postponing action as long as possible' (1960: 104). I have suggested elsewhere that this anxiety was part of the reason for the problem of very lengthy court proceedings regarding the care of children. In researching this topic it often seemed to me that these proceedings with their endless postponements and re-assessments were a way the professionals involved could put off making an unpalatable choice between returning a child to a home where they might come to harm, or separating the child from his or her family on a long-term basis (see, for instance, Beckett and McKeigue, 2003; Taylor et al., 2008; Beckett and Dickens, 2014), the result being that children had to spend long periods in temporary placements, sometimes for a quite significant proportion of their childhood, waiting to learn where that childhood would be spent.

To return to the supervision context, supervisees who seem stuck in Analysis may be afraid of equally unpalatable decisions. They may also be reluctant to confront people whom they have grown fond of, or are intimidated by, or feel sorry for, with a plan that will cause them great distress. Jane Wonnacott notes that 'the supervisee who tends to cope by keeping emotions under control may become stuck in "analysis" where the predominant requirement is intellectualisation rather than emotional engagement' (2012: 162).

Stuck in Action

Supervisees who are stuck in Action, compulsively *do things* while being very resistant to thinking about why, or whether this really is the best plan of action, or whether it might even be better to do nothing at all. High levels of anxiety about a situation, coupled with fears about not being able to work out what is really going on, or fears about being ineffective, often feed into a need to at least be *doing something.* Supervisors too may be stuck in this pattern, if they constantly short-circuit reflection and analysis in the way discussed above. I'd suggest that being 'stuck in Action' is also something we can often see happening at the institutional level: in the form of what has become known as 'the politician's fallacy' or 'the politician's syllogism' (Wikipedia, n.d.):

1. We must do something
2. This is something
3. Therefore, we must do this.

This formulation came originally from the 1980s TV comedy series, *Yes, Minister!*. The fallacy, of course, lies in the fact that there's no point in doing things unless they help and, if you do the wrong thing, it can often be worse than doing nothing at all. In fact you are very *likely* to do the wrong thing, if you have not given sufficient thought to the meaning of the Experience you are reacting to. Ensuring that Experience is given sufficient thought before a decision is made should be important in any field where decisions must be made about complex matters, but perhaps especially important in human services, where the feelings and life experience of the practitioner are likely to be entangled in one way or another with those of her service users.

Unblocking the cycle

Awareness of the possibility that a supervisee may be stuck at some point in the cycle (and indeed the possibility that sometimes the supervisor may be stuck!) is the first step to becoming unstuck. How this is done will depend on the particular circumstances, but if we recognise that anxiety about moving on to other parts of the cycle lies at the heart of being stuck, it becomes possible to use supervision to address that anxiety or to confront it, by asking appropriate questions or even by naming what is going on: 'You seem very reluctant to avoid talking about your feelings about this case', 'I notice that you seem very happy to discuss what's going on in this family, but don't seem to want to explore the actions we might take' etc. Being 'stuck' can be a kind of 'game' in the sense that we use that word in Chapter 7, and there is further discussion there about how to get 'unstuck.' (Short-circuiting the cycle could also be seen in this way.)

DIFFERENT KINDS OF QUESTION

No amount of information about a situation can tell you what you ought to do about it unless you interpret it in some way, so it is not strictly the case that you can jump straight from Experience to Action. The danger is that, unless a little time is set aside for Reflection and Analysis, Action will be based on extremely rudimentary thinking which is full of biases and misapprehensions of one kind or another. This is true not only of supervision, but of any decision-making process. Supervision is, or ought to be, a somewhat more formal and deliberate version of the process that we should go through when making any significant decision. The reason it needs to be more formal and deliberate is that the kinds of decisions that flow from it may have long-lasting, and sometimes even lifelong consequences.

It is because of its importance, that I come back to the supervisory cycle in more detail in Chapters 5 and 6. For the present, I will just add that I am not suggesting here that every item on the supervision agenda necessarily requires detailed and step-by-step progression through the four stages of the cycle. The supervisee may well arrive at a session having done much of this work already. The key point is that Experience requires careful processing before it can become a guide for action and that this processing has several distinct elements (four of them, if you choose to follow this model), each of which involves a different kind of question (see Table 2.2). Supervision ought to include all of these types of question, and important decisions about action plans shouldn't go ahead until all these kinds of question have been explored.

Table 2.2 Different types of questions for different stages/elements in the supervision process, using the 'elements' developed by Tony Morrison and Jane Wonnacott (Wonnacott, 2012)

Supervision stage/element	Examples of questions
Experience	'What's happened on this case since we last met?'
	'What did Mrs X say when you went to visit her?'
	'What sort of state is Mr Y's house in?'
	'What did Dr Q say when you met?'
	'What kind of injuries did Z have?'
Reflection	'How worried are you about this case?'
	'What are your feelings about Mrs X?'
	'Why do you think you are so particularly concerned about Mr Y?'
	'How did you feel when you left the house?'
	'Why do you keep focusing on Mrs X when we talk about the X family, and hardly ever mention the other family members by name?'
Analysis	'Who has the power in this family?'
	'What do you see as the risks to Z in the current situation?'
	'What needs are going unmet for M in the situation as it stands?'
	'Who can N draw on for support?'
	'Why does this family find it so difficult to change?'
Action Planning	'What can we do to reduce the immediate risks to Z?'
	'What needs to happen in order for M's needs to be met?'
	'What do we need to do to make it possible for Mr Y to be reasonably safe at home?'
	'Whose help do we need to enlist at this point, and how?'
	'What further information do we need to decide whether our current thinking is on the right lines?'

CONCLUDING NOTES FOR SUPERVISORS AND SUPERVISEES

Notes for supervisors (including practice educators)

In this chapter, I have drawn attention to the fact that supervision performs a number of different functions and serves the interests of a number of different parties and a number of different agendas. The point of this exercise has been to draw attention to the fact that, unless we keep a watch on our own practice, we may concentrate overmuch on some functions and agendas at the expense of others, perhaps the ones that we find more comfortable.

Drawing on the four 'elements' of the 4 × 4 × 4 model, the second half of the chapter moved on to look at the different processes that take place within the cycle of supervision as it moves from discussion of what is going on in cases to action plans for the future. These four elements will be the subject of more detailed discussion in Chapters 5 and 6. It's particularly important to get hold of the idea that supervision can quite easily short-circuit the four elements and to be aware of the possibility that you as a supervisor may be tempted to do this for a variety of reasons. This kind of short-circuiting results in inferior decisions but also, and crucially, denies supervisees the opportunities to develop their own thinking and decision-making skills.

Recognising that different kinds of question are associated with each element, and consciously ensuring that all four types of question are part of your supervisory practice is a way of avoiding this.

The idea of the supervisee being 'stuck' at various points in the cycle is also an important idea. Once we get hold of the notion that a supervisee may be stuck at a particular stage, we can begin to address the other stages which the supervisee is, for whatever reason, anxious to skip over or to avoid.

Notes for supervisees (including students on placement)

This chapter has set out the range of areas that supervision ought to be expected to cover, first in terms of 'functions', then in terms of 'stakeholders' or beneficiaries or agendas, and finally in terms of the four elements of the supervision cycle as you move from discussing what has been happening on a case (Experience) to an action plan. If you find some of these are missing from your supervision, you may need to ask for them.

You should be aware that part of the problem can be you. If you don't reveal your feelings, your supervisor will find it more difficult to talk about them with you. If you don't offer ideas and expect your supervisor to do all the thinking, you are depriving yourself of a chance to develop your own thinking skills. It is true that your supervisor should challenge you, but you can also ask to be challenged.

CHAPTER SUMMARY

This chapter has looked at what is involved in supervision in a number of different ways. Firstly it looked at the functions of supervision, which are defined in various ways by different writers. It then looked at the 'stakeholders' of supervision, which is to say those who have an interest of some kind in what happens in supervision, given the role of supervision in determining what practitioners do, what they notice and what they prioritise. Another way of looking at this, I suggested, was to look at the different agendas that supervision served.

For the remainder of the chapter I looked at the 'elements' of supervision, using the terms introduced by Morrison (2005) and Wonnacott (2012) for different stages or components of the supervision cycle itself: Experience, Reflection, Analysis, Action Planning. I discussed how the cycle could be short-circuited and why this was something to avoid in most circumstances, and I discussed how the cycle might get blocked at one or other stage, and why this might happen. The chapter concluded with some thoughts on how each stage or element of the supervision cycle has its own characteristic type of question. The next chapter will look at some of the different forms that supervision can take to address specific contexts or specific needs.

3

ALTERNATIVE FORMS OF SUPERVISION

CONTENTS

The last chapter looked at many different aspects of supervision, both in terms of the purposes and interests it serves, and in terms of the processes that take place within a supervision session. In this chapter I want to acknowledge that supervision can also take many different forms. While this book as a whole looks mainly at a kind of supervision that combines accountability supervision and clinical supervision elements and takes place within a one-to-one meeting, it's important to remember that other forms exist and may be useful as supplements or even alternatives.

FORMAL AND INFORMAL SUPERVISION

Many kinds of consultation can and do take place outside of planned supervision sessions, both between the supervisee and her designated supervisor, and between the supervisee and others to whom she turns for advice, or to 'let off steam', or for an opportunity to check out her own thinking, whether because the supervisor is not available, or because the supervisee does not think that the supervisor will be able to help. Not all of these consultations can be described as 'supervision'. They may be fairly perfunctory and practical ('Who do I need to get hold of to get funding for X?'), or they may shade into something more like friendly support (as when a practitioner asks a colleague for a bit of time to help her collect herself after a difficult visit), but, if they are fairly in-depth and are focused on trying to understand a particular situation, these ad hoc consultations do become a form of supervision.

However, as Hawkins and Shohet note (2012: 72), there are some dangers attached to this kind of informal supervision. Unplanned discussions with your supervisor are of course often necessary as new events unfold, but too much reliance on 'supervision on the wing' can mean that less dramatic aspects of the supervisee's work are never properly looked at, and, as Jane Wonnacott points out, ongoing developmental needs may not be addressed (2012: 65). Informal consultations with colleagues can have additional drawbacks. Good supervision entails consciously moving away from some of the normal rules of human interaction because, to do supervision properly, it may be necessary to be challenging or intrusive in ways that, in a social context, might seem impolite. But we tend to support our friends' choices, and take their side in disputes, and so if you ask a colleague who happens to be a friend whether she agrees that you should take such-and-such course of action on such-and-such case, she may be inclined, in the spirit of supportiveness, to reassure you that what you are planning is an excellent idea, rather in the way that she might assure you that your new hairstyle suits you. Similarly, if you express frustration about someone ('X') who is making your life difficult, your colleague-friend may be inclined to agree with you about the awfulness of X, and reassure you that the problem is entirely X's fault, rather than exploring with you how you may be contributing to the problem.

A kind of 'groupthink' (Janis, 1982) can easily build up between colleagues in which they develop a cosy sense that they are right and the 'others' are wrong, thereby reducing anxieties about their decisions and helping each other feel good about themselves, but seriously impairing their ability to come to balanced judgements. (There will be more on 'groupthink' in Chapter 5.) This sort of thing can occur in formal supervision sessions too, but there are increased risks of it happening in an informal setting (a) because of the absence of structure, (b) because the colleague being consulted may be busy and keen to get on to the next thing, and (c) because if you choose who you are going to ask for advice and support, you may be inclined to pick someone who you know will be encouraging and reassuring, rather than someone who might be challenging, or ask awkward questions.

In short, as Hawkins and Shohet put it, 'It is easy to use these less structured types of supervision to avoid the rigours and concentrated focus of regular, formal individual sessions' (2012: 72). This is not to say that informal supervision does not have a part to play, but, when the topic being discussed is a substantial one, informal supervision needs to follow similar rules to formal supervision. An agreed amount of time needs to be set aside, and the person doing the supervising needs to be able to challenge the supervisee in a way that properly interrogates the currently known facts and impressions presented by the supervisee, the supervisee's feelings, and the supervisee's theories and judgements about what is going on. In other words, there needs to be space, and willingness on both sides, for the full supervisory cycle to take place as discussed in Chapter 2, and both parties will need to understand and agree that this is what is to happen. Informal supervision, therefore, needs to become formal if it is to be used to work on problems of any complexity.

Where informal supervision involves someone other than the designated supervisor, and where that someone has no line management responsibility for the supervisee, it is important also to avoid a kind of splitting taking place between the designated supervisor who has managerial responsibility and the informal supervisor who does not, since this would undermine the authority of the designated supervisor, and weaken the line of accountability between the supervisee and her line manager. So again, if 'informal' supervision is to become a regular thing, it really needs to become, in many respects, 'formal', in the sense of having a clear structure and clear boundaries which have been agreed by the formal supervisor.

EXERCISE 3.1

Supplementary supervision for a specific task

George's supervisor and line manager is Tina. However, he is about to embark on a piece of work with a family where the parents are in danger of having their children taken into care unless they can improve their functioning. The work George wants to do would involve using some techniques derived from systemic family work. Tina has no expertise in that area, but another team member, Hamid, has trained as a systemic family therapist and uses systemic ideas in his work all the time. George would very much like to be able to get some supervision from Hamid on this particular piece of work and Hamid is happy to provide it. How should this be arranged so that it will be properly rigorous supervision, and will not undermine the line management accountability between George and Tina?

I would suggest that in the above scenario there first needs to be a three-way discussion between George, Tina and Hamid. There needs to be understanding between all three as to what Hamid will offer, both in terms of time and in terms of content, but there also needs to be an understanding between them about Tina's involvement and George's responsibilities to Tina. If Tina is Hamid's manager as well as George's, she may need to help him create time in his caseload to take on this task, and she should satisfy herself that the working relationship between George and Hamid will be a rigorous and professional one, rather than cosy or collusive. Tina is in a sense subcontracting part of her supervisory responsibilities to Hamid, but she has not handed them over. It is still her responsibility to ensure that the supervision is done properly, and she will still be accountable for the work done by George under Hamid's supervision.

The three of them might agree that George meet with Hamid regularly to discuss the family and to consider questions and interventions that George could use in the sessions. However, bearing in mind that the reason for the work is that there are concerns about the parents' ability to meet the children's needs, Tina would need to be involved in any decision about whether the family had reached the threshold where legal proceedings were needed, or indeed any decision about whether they were now functioning well enough to be able to withdraw. So there would need to be a clear understanding that both George and Hamid must report to Tina if there is any new information that might be salient to threshold decisions of that kind, and there would need to continue to be regular input on this case from Tina, so she would be in a position to form her own judgement on this.

PEER SUPERVISION

The proposed arrangement between Hamid and George in the exercise above is an example of peer supervision: supervision between professional colleagues with no line management relationship. (As I noted in Chapter 1, in some professions, this may be the norm.) Many informal consultations that take place between peers may shade into a form of peer supervision, but as I noted in the previous section, if peer supervision is to deal with complex issues, then it really needs to be formalised. A chat is not the same thing as a supervision session.

Hawkins and Shohet observe that peer supervision may be necessary in some contexts where the line manager has 'neither the time nor the ability to supervise' (2012: 191). I said in Chapter 1 that many managers focus much more on, and are perhaps much more confident with, accountability supervision as opposed to clinical supervision, and, where this is the case, supervisees may feel that they do not have enough clinical supervision. Peer supervision, whether it is done individually (perhaps on a reciprocal basis) or in a group, can help to fill a gap of this kind, and meet the need for a form of supervision that looks at how you work and how you think, and doesn't just address your adherence to targets and procedures. However, the cautionary notes which I struck above about 'informal' arrangements all apply here. Citing Gaie Houston (1985), Hawkins and Shohet identify a number of 'games' (see Chapter 7) that can be played out in peer group supervision sessions, and which can render them dysfunctional. One of these is the game called '*We are all so wonderful*':

> Peer group members can avoid having their anxieties about being criticized or found out by heaping fulsome praise on other peer members as an unacknowledged payment for returning the favour. This becomes a covert form of a 'protection racket'. (Hawkins and Shohet, 2012: 192–3)

This game could also be described as a manifestation of groupthink, one of whose characteristics is overestimation of the group (Janis, 1982). A related game is '*Ain't it awful*', in which 'the peer group sits around, reinforcing each other's sense of powerlessness' (Hawkins and Shohet, 2012: 193):

> One variant of ['*Ain't it awful*'] is to spend the time sharing how you must be mad to work for this 'authority' or 'hospital'. Another variant is for [practitioners] to spend their time showing how clients are hateful, vicious and manipulative beings who resist your best endeavours at every attempt. (Hawkins and Shohet, 2012: 193)

Again, this game could be described as a manifestation of groupthink, since a characteristic of groupthink is a tendency to negatively stereotype people outside the group who the group find challenging or threatening.

These kinds of games can happen in formal line management supervision also, but they are more likely to occur in informal and poorly structured contexts because the less clear the purpose or boundaries of a peer supervision session are – whether it takes place one-to-one or in a group – the easier it will be for the session to be captured by some other agenda, such as those illustrated by these games (which are primarily about making members of the group feel better about themselves). Sometimes group meetings may become little more than enjoyable social occasions.

One of the advantages of supervision by a line manager is that the supervisor does actually hold responsibility for the supervisee's work and can be held accountable for mistakes made by the supervisee if these result from decisions agreed in supervision. So the supervisor has a personal stake in making sure she understands what her supervisee is doing. This doesn't apply in the same way to peer supervision.

GROUP SUPERVISION

I have referred to peer group supervision, but group supervision can also take place in a line management context, if a manager (or someone else with supervisory responsibilities, such as a practice educator or a senior practitioner) meets with several supervisees at the same time, and supervisees take turns to be supervised and to contribute ideas to the supervision of others. Jane Wonnacott urges caution about such arrangements, arguing that 'within a group it is possible for more vocal people to dominate and for some cases to slip through the net' (2012: 63). Some participants in a group may also be reluctant to share doubts and uncertainties that they would be willing to talk about in a one-to-one session, and some may abandon their own thinking and take their cue from members of the group they perceive as powerful. Wonnacott's recommendation is that group supervision should supplement individual supervision rather than replace it.

Hawkins and Shohet see both advantages and disadvantages of the group supervision approach. The advantages include 'economies of time, money or expertise' (2012: 178): group supervision may make it possible for supervisees to get access to skilled supervisors who would not have time to see them all individually. Group supervision can also provide 'a supportive atmosphere of peers in which supervisees share anxieties and realise that others are facing similar issues' (2012: 178). Another benefit is that supervisees can get feedback from colleagues as well as the supervisor, meaning that the process may be 'less dominated by the supervisor, with the concurrent dangers of over-influence and dependency' because the whole group contributes ideas, drawing on a wider experience of life experience than an individual supervisor could do, and supervisors themselves can 'test out their emotional and intuitive response to the material by checking if other group members have the same response' (2012: 178). On the downside, groups can succumb to groupthink; group dynamics can be complicated and time-consuming to unravel; group members can be competitive and/or defensive about their work; and there may be issues about confidentiality when personal information about service users is shared with a whole group of colleagues (2012: 179). Clear and explicit rules and boundaries about the scope of the group, its membership, functioning and agenda are very important, and the supervisor needs to be confident about managing the group dynamics.

DIFFERENT PROFESSIONAL CONTEXTS

As discussed in the Introduction to the book, the particular kind of supervision this book addresses is the kind that is necessary in human service organisations, where both clinical supervision and organisational accountability are very important. I noted that, in settings where the users of the service are free to go elsewhere, the accountability side of supervision may be less important. On the other hand, in organisations where the task being performed can be precisely defined and requires technical knowledge rather than people skills, then what we are calling 'clinical supervision' may be less to the fore, but accountability supervision remains important.

I think it is worth coming back to that thought briefly in a chapter on forms of supervision, because the precise form of supervision that is required will depend in part on the nature of the work undertaken. Not only different professions, but different branches of the same profession require a different kind of supervision and different emphases. Child and family social workers, for instance, are frequently in the business of trying to help people to change the way they behave, either because they are putting themselves at risk or are putting others at risk, and, to add to the difficulty of the task, they are often trying to do this with involuntary clients who did not ask for the service in the first place. There are no precise rules about how to do this. Not only is each case different, but each practitioner is different too and brings different skills and personal characteristics to the job.

Social workers in a hospital setting, who are working to help adult patients move out into the community, are also to some extent in the business of helping people change the way they do things (either the patient or the carers or both), but the mix of tools at their disposal tends to include a larger proportion of practical services – day care, residential care, care services and nursing care provided at home – and they must work very closely with other professionals who have more specialist expertise in the patient's illness and its treatment. Their clients may be involuntary in the sense that they may have no one else they can turn to, but as a general rule, their clients will want the help that the social worker is trying to provide and will not think of the social work intervention as something imposed on them. Powerful external drivers for the work, which constantly create tension, include the need to free up hospital beds and the need to keep within budget. This is a very different kind of job, with different pressures and challenges, from that of a child and family social worker, even though both are members of the same profession. And there can obviously be considerably larger differences *between* professions.

Nevertheless, it is not unusual in multi-disciplinary services for a supervisor from one professional discipline to have supervisees from other disciplines or specialisms. A nurse may supervise a social worker, for instance, or vice versa. The challenges this poses depend on the context. In some multi-disciplinary teams, all team members, regardless of their professional background, carry out fairly similar tasks – I think for example of a youth justice team where staff may have social work, probation, police or youth work training but all have roughly the same responsibilities – and, in such a team, the supervisor will probably not have any great difficulty in understanding what supervisees are doing, though she may have some challenges dealing with the different professional ethos and expectations (including expectations of supervision) of people from different professional backgrounds.

However, there are also work units where different team members perform very different, specialised tasks, depending on their professional background. These may be tasks which the supervisor is personally unfamiliar with, and may be carried out using skills and knowledge which the supervisor does not share. This might happen, for instance, if someone with a social work background had responsibility for supervising an occupational therapist.

There are many benefits of inter-professional and multi-disciplinary working. As Allyson Davys and Liz Beddoe (2010: 128) observe, people from different professional backgrounds 'bring their own assumptions, reactions, disciplinary and theoretical orientation, emotional responses and political perspectives' to a given situation – and this can be valuable. A supervisor with a different professional background to her supervisee may ask interesting and challenging questions which a supervisor from the same professional background would not think to ask. And of course there are many commonalities: 'regardless of profession, practitioners often bring the same things to supervision: stress, anxiety, conflict, ethical and moral dilemmas, "stuckness" and so forth' (Beddoe and Davys, 2008: 37). However, rhetoric about commonalities and transferable skills can in my experience serve as a smokescreen that conceals a real problem: a supervisor with a different background cannot necessarily interrogate her supervisee's practice with anything like the same rigour as she could interrogate the practice of a supervisee who is doing a job she herself is familiar with.

In a former role, I supervised mainly child and family social workers, which was my own background, but for a time also had responsibility for supervising a few social workers in a special unit which worked exclusively with adults suffering from dementia, a field of which I had almost no experience. Even though the dementia specialists came from my own profession, I have to admit I privately questioned whether I was really contributing anything to their work, other than (hopefully) making them feel vaguely supported, because I was not personally familiar with the issues they had to deal with, or the colleagues and agencies that they worked with, or even with the dynamics of their multi-disciplinary team, which was situated in a building a couple of miles away from the office where I was based.

When the supervisor has only a general, external sort of understanding of the work she is supposed to be supervising, this creates challenges from a managerial/accountability point of view: how does a social worker supervising an occupational therapist know that the OT is doing a good job, and how can she be truly answerable for what the OT does, if she herself would not know how to do that job? And it creates challenges also from a professional/clinical point of view: how does a social worker being supervised by a nurse get the in-depth interrogation of her professional practice that she needs, if the nurse has only a fairly general understanding of the social worker's role and no experience at all of performing it?

DELEGATED SUPERVISION

My suggestion here is that both supervisors and supervisees in such a context need to think about what supervisory needs can be met by their supervision sessions (see Table 3.1), and what needs, realistically, may have to be met in other ways. The supervisor may be able to reduce any deficit by learning more about her supervisee's profession, and getting to know the other professionals with whom her supervisee works, but this only goes so far. It may make sense to build in some form of peer supervision arrangement for the supervisee, or consultation with another manager from the same profession or specialism as the supervisee.

As discussed after Exercise 3.1 above, recruiting others to contribute to the supervision of one's supervisee is not necessarily a dereliction of one's own responsibility as a supervisor, provided that the arrangement is properly set up. It can be a way of discharging one's responsibilities. And, as Exercise 3.1 illustrated, it can be appropriate to delegate supervision in this way, even when supervisee and supervisor come from the same field, if there is a particular piece of work to be supervised which requires more specialist knowledge than the supervisor can provide.

Table 3.1 Questions for supervisors and supervisees with different professional backgrounds

	For the Supervisor	For the Supervisee
Questions about managerial supervision	How do I know what kind of job my supervisee is doing? What control do I have over what my supervisee is doing? What managerial tasks can I perform in relation to my supervisee and what, if any, do I need help with? What needs to happen for me to be confident that my supervisee's work is being properly overseen?	Can my supervisor share responsibility for my work when she doesn't understand what I do as well as I do? If not, what are the deficits and what needs to happen in order to feel that someone is genuinely sharing some responsibility for my work?
Questions about professional supervision	How can I help my supervisee with her practice when my knowledge of her area of work is more limited than hers? What kind of support with her job can I provide for my supervisee, and what, if any, can I not provide? What needs to happen in order to ensure that my supervisee receives the kind of professional support she needs to do her job as well as possible and to develop her skills?	Does my supervisor understand my work well enough to be able to challenge me, notice my bad habits, help me resolve the things I find difficult and recognise the things I do well? Do I feel supported by my supervisor, and if not, where are the deficits and what needs to happen in order to let me have the opportunity to think about my practice?

CONCLUDING NOTES FOR SUPERVISORS AND SUPERVISEES

Notes for supervisors (including practice educators)

Different styles of supervision are appropriate depending on the kind of task being discussed.

Sometimes supervisors may find that their supervisee is engaged in a task of which they have very limited understanding. In these circumstances it is entirely appropriate to arrange for your supervisee to have supervision from someone else (for instance from a team colleague). Since this supervision is delegated, and you continue to have line management and supervisory responsibility, it's important that there is a properly discussed agreement between the three parties as to how such an arrangement will work, and how you as the main supervisor will be kept informed. In situations where you have line management responsibility for someone from a completely different field or profession, these kinds of delegated arrangements may need to be ongoing.

Your supervisees will of course from time to time seek advice from their colleagues as well as from you, but you will need to keep an eye on any parallel supervision arrangement that runs the risk of by-passing you altogether. Alternative supervision arrangements need to have the same kind of rigour as more formal supervision, and should not be a cosier and less demanding alternative.

Group supervision can be a valuable option, but there are drawbacks which may create more problems than it's worth if you are not confident in managing groups.

Notes for supervisees (including students on placement)

Your designated supervisor may not always provide the supervision you need, either because she doesn't have the time, or because she isn't sufficiently familiar with the task you are seeking supervision on. But always bear in mind that, if you don't seem to be getting the supervision you need, the problem might in part be you. Have you told the supervisor what you want? Are you being open with your supervisor about the aspects of the job you're having difficulty with? Is your dissatisfaction with your supervisor due in part to your supervisor confronting you with things that you need to face but would prefer not to?

Of course, you always have the option of asking others for advice, but beware of 'groupthink', and do not choose others to talk to just because you know they will tell you what you want to hear. Sometimes it may be necessary to set up some kind of more formal supervision arrangement with someone other than your designated supervisor, which should be arranged with your designated supervisor's agreement.

CHAPTER SUMMARY

This chapter has looked at different forms of supervision that may supplement or even sometimes replace the one-to-one, clinical/accountability supervision discussed in the previous two chapters.

I have looked at informal supervision, whether from the designated supervisor or others, which takes place outside of regular supervision sessions, and have cautioned against confusing a supportive chat with supervision. Even informal supervision needs rules and boundaries. This discussion segued into consideration specifically of peer supervision, whether one-to-one or in a group, where supervision comes from a colleague or colleagues of the supervisee rather than the line manager.

I considered group supervision in which a supervisor meets with several supervisees together, noting the advantages (richer variety of experience, different perspectives ...) and disadvantages (possible 'groupthink' and other complicated group dynamics).

I then moved on to discuss the special case of supervision where supervisor and supervisee have different areas of expertise or come from different professions, noting that, while there is value in such supervision and sometimes even advantages, there may well be a deficit in that the supervisor may not have enough detailed knowledge of the supervisee's work to be able to thoroughly interrogate her thinking and practice. And this led on to a short discussion of delegated supervision arrangements, which had already been touched on in Exercise 3.1.

The next chapter will look at the authority of the supervisor, what it consists of, and how it interacts with the personalities of the supervisor and supervisee.

4

POWER AND AUTHORITY

CONTENTS

Imagine yourself back at school for a moment and think about your teachers at the time. I hope you can remember at least some teachers that you and your fellow-pupils liked and respected, but you will probably remember others who you didn't rate so highly. Probably you can recall some teachers who were overly negative or punitive, and some who were just uninterested. Perhaps, too, there were some – young and inexperienced teachers perhaps – who seemed desperate to 'get down with the kids' and didn't want you to think of them as part of the system at all. But my guess is that the ones you remember as the best teachers were those who were comfortable with their authority and able to use it, but were also able to communicate warmth and interest. My suggestion here is that this ability to own and be comfortable with authority while also being engaged and supportive is an important attribute, not only in teaching, but in many professions, as well as in other roles such as parenting where caring and controlling roles are necessarily combined. I will refer to this quality as 'being *authoritative*' which, as we'll see, is a different thing from being *authoritarian*. It is key to being a good supervisor.

ABOUT POWER

My own profession of social work has an uneasy relationship with power. (Whether this is true of other professions, I leave to members of those professions to decide.) Most social workers see themselves as being on the side of the powerless against the powerful, but social workers are frequently involved in exercising a good deal of power over the powerless themselves. One way that social workers sometimes deal with this is to try in various ways to conceal, or distance themselves from, the power that it is part of their job to exercise (see Svensson, 2009, for more on this). This is the approach of the 'down with the kids' teacher, who tries to persuade his pupils that he's on their side against the system. The opposite approach is to become over-fond of the exercise of power: In a focus group in which I was involved, social workers spoke disapprovingly of a colleague who had said to a client with a snap of her fingers: 'I can take your baby away just like that' (Taylor et al., 2008: 26). But good social workers, like good teachers, and indeed good parents, are able to own their own power while still being able to make their service users feel supported and appreciated. And my suggestion is that supervisors should aim to achieve something similar to this in relation to their supervisees.

In an old, but still very frequently cited model, French and Raven (1959) suggested that power came from five different sources which I'll list with my own explanations:

1 *Coercion:* Power derived from the ability to force people to comply
2 *Reward:* Power derived from the ability give or withhold rewards of one kind or another
3 *Legitimacy:* Power derived from the perception of others that you are in a legitimate position of authority

4 *Expert:* Power derived from the perception that you have special expertise
5 *Referent:* Power derived from your perceived personal qualities, which includes what is called charisma and personal authority.

A supervisor possesses some of these forms of power simply by virtue of her job. Coercive powers are unlikely to be used but they are implicit in, for instance, the supervisor's disciplinary responsibilities. Reward power lies in the ability of the supervisor to make things both easier and more difficult for the supervisee, and perhaps also (depending on the precise nature of the supervisor's job), the ability to access resources which supervisees need. In the case of practice teachers, the reward power lies in the ability of the teacher to pass or fail the placement. Legitimate power comes from the recognition on the part of (most) supervisees that the supervisor has a right to oversee, challenge and, if necessary, direct their work by virtue of her position. (I should note, by the way, that, although these sources of power come with the job, this is not to say that every supervisor is equally confident about exercising them.)

Supervisors do not *necessarily* possess Expert power in that they may not be any more experienced or skilful than their supervisees (and may be less so). Even so, they do bring to supervision the benefits of a more detached viewpoint which means that they can see things that the supervisee fails to see, and this in itself, properly handled, can be a kind of Expert power even if the supervisor is no more skilled a practitioner than the supervisee. (Supervision itself, in other words, is a skill which can confer Expert power.) The extent to which supervisors possess Referent power will depend on their personalities and their experience as supervisors, but as a supervisor grows comfortable and confident in her role, her Referent power is likely to increase. However, supervisees may well also have Referent power – there are some very confident and charismatic practitioners who have chosen not to move into supervisory or management positions precisely because they know they are good at their jobs – as well as having Expert power. To the extent that the supervisor wants her supervisees to think well of her, supervisees also have Reward power, particularly those supervisees who the supervisor most respects, in the sense that the supervisor may seek reassurance from them, and be pleased when reassurance is given.

Many people moving into a supervisory position for the first time will be uneasy about the power they are now supposed to have. They may experience 'impostor syndrome' or they may worry that they will be seen as, so to speak, 'going over to the dark side'. To deal with these anxieties they may adopt strategies such as the 'down with the kids' approach, or its opposite, the over-controlling approach, as a way of addressing these anxieties (there will be more on this in Chapter 7). It is helpful in this situation for supervisors to remind themselves of how they addressed the exact same problem when they first became practitioners. How did they 'own' the authority inherent in their new position while still remaining helpful and supportive?

The following are some questions to ask yourself about your own relationship with power. (If you are not a supervisor, you might like to ask yourself questions in connection with your relationship with your service users.)

EXERCISE 4.1

You and power

- Above I have listed five 'sources' of power. Which of these do you feel most confident about? Which do you feel least confident about and why?
- If you don't feel entirely confident, how do you deal with this? Are you prone to try and minimise the power difference between yourself and those you supervise, or do you over-compensate by emphasising your power, or pretending to possess power that deep down you don't feel that you have?
- Thinking back over your experience of being in a subordinate position to others, what role models do you have that you would wish to emulate, and what role models would you wish to avoid?

Anxieties about power can be divided into, firstly, anxieties about whether or not you *have* power, and secondly, anxieties about how to *exercise* the power you have. In the first case, I am sure that many new supervisors worry about whether they have sufficient expertise to be able to supervise the work of others, in much the same way that many new practitioners worry about whether they have sufficient expertise to be able to offer anything useful to service users. Certainly, when I first became a supervisor I was acutely aware that several of the social workers I was to supervise were much more experienced and skilled than I was, and more than I would ever be in some cases.

My suggestion, though, is that the new supervisor needs to relax and resist the urge to try and compensate in some way for their lack of Expert power. Just as new social workers (and practitioners of other professions) need to learn just to listen to their clients and not feel they have to come up with all the answers, so new supervisors need to remember that (as I noted above), their detached position is in itself valuable and that they do not need to be better practitioners than their supervisees in order to be useful. It is *not* necessary to come up with all the answers to be a good supervisor. In fact, on the contrary (and as discussed in Chapter 2), a good supervisor should encourage supervisees to come up with the answers.

The second anxiety, about exercising the power you do have, may present itself as a dilemma: how to be supportive to your staff while at the same time insisting on a high standard of work?

RESPONSIVENESS AND DEMANDINGNESS

Muayyad Jabri (2012: 56) offers the quadrant in Figure 4.1 to represent different styles of management.

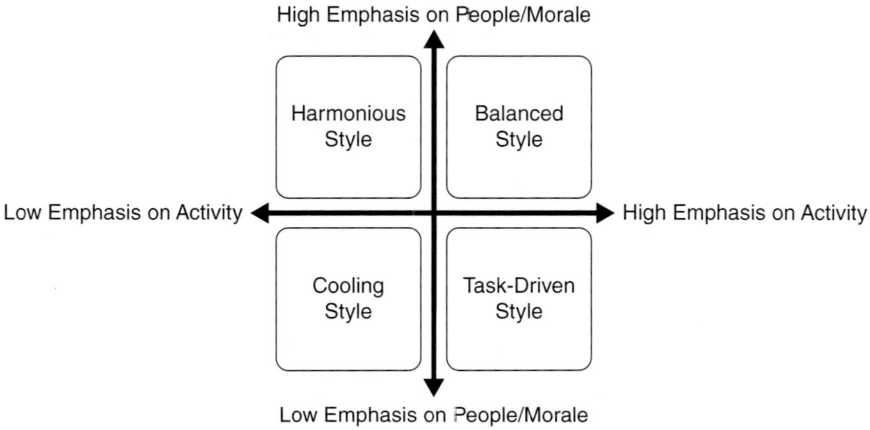

Figure 4.1 Task orientation versus people (morale) orientation (after Jabri, 2012, reproduced with permission of Red Globe Press)

In this diagram the horizontal axis represents emphasis on activity (task orientation), ranging from low emphasis on the left to high emphasis on the right, while the vertical axis represents emphasis on people/morale, ranging from high at the top to low at the bottom. So, by combining these two axes, we get a 'harmonious' style where the manager is more interested in keeping morale high than in getting stuff done, a 'task-driven' style where the manager is more interested in getting the task done than in looking after the staff, and a 'balanced' style where the manager works on both morale and task delivery. The fourth quadrant, the 'cooling' style, is what you get when a manager doesn't work on either supporting staff or getting the job done.

What immediately strikes me about this quadrant is its similarity to another quadrant that will be familiar to many professionals working with families. Baumrind's (1978) parenting styles quadrant is based on the two dimensions of demandingness (roughly equivalent to Jabri's 'activity emphasis') and responsiveness (roughly equivalent to Jabri's 'people/morale emphasis'). As shown in Figure 4.2, I have reversed the Baumrind quadrant left-to-right from the way it is normally shown, in order to bring out the similarity with the Jabri quadrant. (If you are a social worker, you may notice that the two dimensions 'demandingness' and 'responsiveness' also correspond quite well to what are often described as the two distinct aspects of the social work role: care and control.)

So here we have a 'permissive' style of parenting in which parents are responsive but undemanding. (One might also call it 'indulgent'.) We have an 'authoritarian' style of parenting in which parents are demanding but unresponsive. We have a 'neglectful'

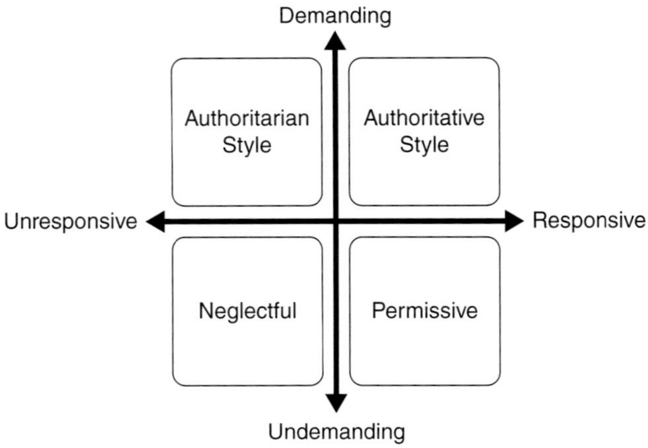

Figure 4.2 Baumrind's parenting styles (after Baumrind, 1978)

style of parenting in which parents are neither responsive nor demanding. And finally, we have an 'authoritative' style of parenting in which parents are both demanding and responsive.

As the comparison with Jabri's quadrant illustrates, and as Wonnacott (2012: 74) has noted long before me, Baumrind's model is applicable not just to parenting styles but to any caring relationship. Thus, if you think again about the teachers I asked you to recall at the beginning of the chapter, you will probably find that you can fit them quite easily into this quadrant. The 'get down with the kids' teacher, who tries to be popular by abdicating authority, belongs in the 'permissive' quadrant. The controlling, punitive teacher belongs in the 'authoritarian' quadrant. The teacher who does the bare minimum necessary to get through the day belongs in the 'neglectful' quadrant. But my guess is that the teachers who you most admired, and who taught you the most, were in the 'authoritative' quadrant. I'm thinking now of a history teacher in my children's school who was very much liked and admired by the students. He was very warm and very supportive of his students, but he wouldn't take any nonsense from them and certainly never tried to pretend that he was one of them.

Parents whose own childhood experiences were not entirely happy will often try to compensate by deliberately parenting their children in a different way, but sometimes they fail to recognise that there are two distinct dimensions involved: responsiveness *and* demandingness. Parents who are determined not to be 'authoritarian' may become 'permissive', thus correcting their own parents' absence of responsiveness, but failing to recognise that demandingness, of itself, is not a bad thing, provided that it is accompanied by care. And in the same way, supervisors and managers who are determined to get either the 'responsiveness' or the 'demandingness' aspect of their job right may fail to recognise the importance of the other dimension. The challenge lies in *combining* responsiveness and demandingness, just as the challenge for a social worker, or a teacher, or a youth worker, lies in combining care and control.

EXERCISE 4.2

The Supervision Styles Quadrant

1. What does an 'authoritarian' supervisor look like? How about a 'permissive' supervisor, or a 'neglectful' one? What does an 'authoritative' supervisor look like? (It's possible, of course, that some supervisors adopt different styles depending on whom they are supervising: 'Permissive', perhaps, with a supervisee they find intimidating, 'authoritarian' with a supervisee who they find exasperating … etc.)
2. Using the four headings in the Baumrind quadrant, try to locate the supervisors you have experienced yourself (or, if you have had no previous supervisors, try to locate other people who have been in a position of authority over you). Bear in mind that some people may be in between two sections of the quadrant so that you might end up with something like Figure 4.3, with different supervisors indicated by the letters A to E.
3. Where would you place yourself as a supervisor? Or, if you are not a supervisor, where would you place yourself as a practitioner?
4. Which dimension do you find hardest: getting 'demandingness' right, or getting 'responsiveness' right? (In Jabri's terms: do you find the 'people/morale' side of things easier or harder than the 'getting stuff done' ('activity'/'task') side of things?)

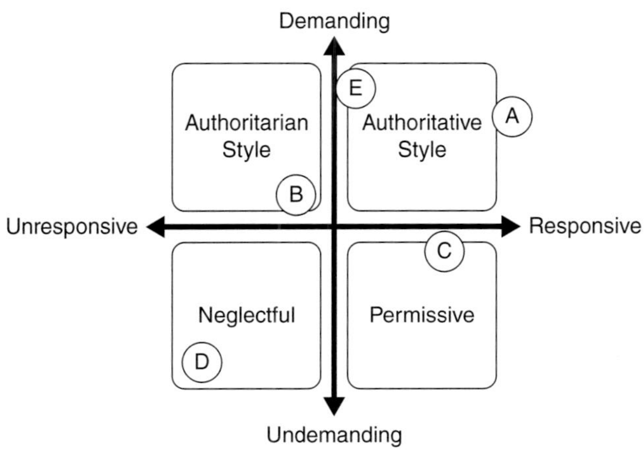

Figure 4.3 Example of a Baumrind-style chart completed for previous supervisors A–E (or for others in authority, if no previous supervisors)

For some supervisors the 'responsiveness' aspect comes naturally – they are very good at making their staff feel supported, and at maintaining the morale of the team – but the 'demandingness' aspect involves going against the grain – they are not so good at making sure that work gets done to the right standard and in the right timeframe.

For some, the opposite is true. However, since looking after the staff and getting the job done are both important – and indeed ultimately you can't achieve one without the other – it's important that supervisors challenge themselves, and make themselves work at whichever part of the job comes less naturally to them, because good supervisors need to be in the 'authoritative' corner of the quadrant. But that is not to say that all supervisors need to work in exactly the same kind of way. You have to be authoritative in the way that works for you. This means understanding why some aspects of your role are easier for you than others, and knowing your own strengths and weaknesses.

AUTHORITY AND PERSONAL DRIVERS

Why is it that different parts of the job are easier or harder for different people, and why do different people have to do the job in different ways? A useful idea here, I have found, is the idea of drivers. Hay (2009: 73) cites five drivers as follows:

- I will be OK if I am perfect
- I will be OK if I am strong
- I will be OK if I hurry up
- I will be OK if I please you
- I will be OK if I try hard

These drivers originate from the field of Transactional Analysis and specifically from a paper by Kahler and Capers (1974: 32) who assert that 'Observations of several thousand people strongly suggest that there are five – and only five – basic counter-script drivers.' It is not my intention to assert that there are necessarily *only* these five (which strikes me as debatable) or indeed to explore the theoretical background in any detail. The points I want to focus on for the present purposes are, firstly, the idea that most of us in childhood internalise certain messages – or 'scripts' – about what we must do to be 'OK', and secondly, the idea that we do not all internalise the *same* messages, and therefore do not all have the same drivers.

Our drivers are prone to trap us into particular patterns of thinking and behaving, but in a work context it is perhaps more helpful to recognise that (as noted by Gallop and Hafford-Letchfield, 2012: 29–31) each driver confers both advantages and disadvantages. For instance, a person who needs to 'be strong' is good in a crisis, but finds it hard to admit to worries or stress. A 'be strong' supervisor or supervisee may be prone to skip over the 'Reflection' aspect of supervision (using the word in the restrictive sense introduced in Chapter 2), because it involves being willing to discuss feelings and vulnerabilities. A person who needs to 'be perfect' can be relied upon to produce good work, but it may be to a higher (and more time-consuming) standard than is actually sensible or practical with the resources available – and she may also find it difficult to delegate to other people. A person who has internalised the need to 'hurry up' is likely to be a fast worker, but may also cut corners and may be impatient with those who want to take time to think things over. A 'hurry up' supervisor may be prone to 'short-circuit' the supervision cycle in the way discussed in Chapter 2.

A lot of people who go into 'caring professions' like social work have a strong 'please others' driver – we go into the work because we have a need to look after people and make things better for them – and this makes us work hard at getting on with people and being supportive to them. But the downside of it is that we may find it difficult to do things that we know will *displease* people. A supervisor with this driver may be experienced by her staff as supportive and kind, but may find it difficult to do things like challenge people about deficiencies in their work. In other words, responsiveness may come more naturally to her than demandingness and she may, if she is not careful, find herself in the 'permissive' – or indulgent – corner of the quadrant that we have borrowed from Baumrind. A 'be perfect' person, on the other hand, might be more prone to find herself in the 'authoritarian' corner – strong on demandingness, but weak on responsiveness – since her greatest need is not to look after other people but to make sure everything is done absolutely right.

Unless we become aware of our own drivers, we will be prone to assume that they are 'just the way things are' and people with different drivers will seem somewhat mysterious to us or even just downright wrong. But when we are aware of our drivers, it becomes possible to compensate for them. Kahler and Capers (1974: 33) use the term 'allowers' to describe messages which can be used to counteract people's scripts/drivers. Thus their 'allower' for 'hurry up' is 'It's OK to take your time', the 'allower' for 'be strong' is 'It's OK to be open (and to take care of your own needs)' (1974: 33), and the 'allower' for the driver to please others – Kahler and Capers call this the 'please me' driver because it originates in a message received from others – is 'It's OK to consider yourself and respect yourself'. In a supervision context this might translate as 'It's OK to insist on doing your job properly, even if this means upsetting someone.'

EXERCISE 4.3

It's OK to do your job properly

Harriet is the supervisor of Ben. Ben promised in the last supervision session and the one before that to get his recording up to date, but still has not done so. Ben is a likeable and generous person, who has been supportive to Harriet. However, Harriet

(Continued)

is aware that she cannot let Ben go on agreeing to things in supervision and then not doing them. Harriet has a strong need to please people, and finds it very difficult to confront people or to express anger or disappointment that might offend or upset people. But she knows that if she raises the recording backlog in the same gentle way as she did in the two previous sessions, Ben will respond (as before) by being very apologetic, will mention pressure of work, and will promise to do his best to get it done before next supervision. When Ben arrives for supervision he is, as usual, warm and friendly. He asks about Harriet's daughter who has not been well.

1 How might things transpire if Harriet has prepared herself to go against her normal script?
2 How might she prepare herself?

If she doesn't prepare herself, it seems likely that Harriet will essentially do the same thing as she's done in the two previous supervisions: that is she will ask Ben to address the recording issue, but in such a gentle way that Ben doesn't hear it as a high priority. But sooner or later, she may get angry – perhaps angry with herself as much as anything, but also with Ben for making her feel powerless – and react in an unnecessarily aggressive way which will do long-term harm to their working relationship.

On the other hand, if she was aware of her powerful need to please people – aware of it as a script she has learnt, I mean, rather than as a personal weakness to be ashamed of – she could prepare herself for the session. She could remind herself that getting Ben to update his recording isn't just a personal whim, but actually one of the responsibilities of her job and that, if Ben doesn't comply, this could reflect badly on her as well as on him. She could also remind herself that Ben is a nice person but is busy, and therefore constantly having to prioritise his work. So, unless he's made to feel that catching up on recording really *is* a high priority he may continue to leave it on his 'to do' list. It's not her job to be aggressive, and it wouldn't be helpful, but she does need to set aside her need to please Ben and to insist in an authoritative way on him completing his recording. She needs him to know she means business and won't let this drop. Perhaps she could ask to see his diary and agree with him a time he will set aside to do it. Perhaps she could arrange a time before the next scheduled supervision session when she will expect him to show her that his recording is up to date. Both of these would be reasonable requests, and well within her rights, but Ben won't like it, and she may need to consciously give herself permission to be firm and to resist, for the moment, her need to please people.

How precisely Harriet handles Ben's reluctance to get his recording done, will be linked not only to Harriet's personality, or her scripts, but also to Ben's. It is helpful if supervisors are able to recognise not just their own personal drivers but those of their supervisees, so they can, if need be, address them. Sometimes one of the tasks of a supervisor may be to offer 'allowers', as discussed above, to help supervisees too much in the grip of a particular driver. A 'try hard' supervisee, for instance, may feel a constant need to take new initiatives and come up with new ideas, and her supervisor may need to remind her that it's OK just to do a steady competent job and get the ordinary everyday things right.

It's helpful too, if supervisees are similarly aware of the preoccupations of their supervisors. It may sometimes be the case that a supervisee may need to tell a supervisor what kind of feedback she needs. If you have a 'people pleaser' supervisor who is always praising your work and telling you that you are doing fine, you may need to say 'I don't need you to spare my feelings. I'd prefer you to be honest. I want you to tell me what I could do better!'

But it's also worth thinking about the interaction between the personality of the supervisor and the supervisee. For instance, if we take the five drivers above, there are twenty-five possible permutations as in Figure 4.4. How does supervision work if there are two people pleasers together? How about a 'be strong' supervisee with a people pleaser supervisor, or a 'hurry up' supervisor with a 'be perfect' supervisee?

Supervisor's Drivers

Supervisee's Drivers	Be Perfect	Be Strong	Please Me	Hurry Up	Try Hard
Be Perfect					
Be Strong					
Please Me					
Hurry Up					
Try Hard					

Figure 4.4 Interaction of supervisee's and supervisor's drivers

PERCEPTIONS OF CONFIDENCE AND RELIABILITY

Of course it is not only different combinations of drivers and personality type that result in each supervisory relationship being different. The supervisor's appraisals of the competence, commitment and trustworthiness of the supervisee are, quite appropriately, also factors. As Marion Bogo and Katherine Dill observe:

> When they have concerns about workers' performance and competency issues ... supervisors seem to "shift gears" from a collaborative working relationship to one where their power and authority is an ever-present and tangible aspect of the relationship. (2008: 149)

The degree to which a given supervisor has concerns about a given supervisee will be connected to particular factors in their relationship, but it may also be affected by external factors. Bogo and Dill observe that at times when an agency feels under attack from negative reports in the media, a 'culture of fear' may result in a more controlling approach by supervisors (2008: 148). Since fear is the result of feeling that we are threatened by things that we may not be able to control, it is understandable that fear makes us more controlling, but the fact remains that being over-controlling ('authoritarian' in the terms we used above) can be counterproductive, since it denies learning opportunities to those we try to control. Manzoni and Barsoux (1998, 2002) described what they called the 'set-up-to-fail syndrome' in which attempts by managers to micro-manage staff who were perceived to be failing, proved to be counterproductive because they made the staff member feel even less confident. These authors (who are writing, incidentally, about management in general and not particularly the human services) also identify a widespread tendency of managers to divide their staff into a trusted 'in-crowd' who are given a great deal of freedom in deciding how to operate, and an untrusted 'out-crowd', who are only given simpler tasks and are closely directed on how to perform them. Manzoni and Barsoux observe:

> Labeling is something we all do, because it allows us to function more efficiently. It saves time by providing rough-and-ready guides for interpreting events and interacting with others. Managers, for instance, use categorical thinking to figure out quickly who should get what tasks. That's the good news.
>
> The downside of categorical thinking is that in organizations it leads to premature closure. Having made up his mind about a subordinate's limited ability and poor motivation, a manager is likely to notice supporting evidence while selectively dismissing contrary evidence. (For example, a manager might interpret a terrific new product idea from an out-group subordinate as a lucky onetime event.) Unfortunately for some subordinates, several studies show that bosses tend to make decisions about in-groups and out-groups even as early as five days into their relationships with employees. (Manzoni and Barsoux, 1998)

Social workers in the children and families field, teachers, youth workers and other professionals whose job entails exercising authority over service users, should already be aware of the danger of setting people up to fail. Supervisors can inadvertently do the same thing to supervisees by overly controlling them. (It occurs to me that, in some respects, supervisees can set up supervisors to fail as well: If you refuse to let your supervisor into your thinking, on the basis that you are sure she won't be able to help, then you are in effect preventing her from being a good supervisor.)

This is not to deny that a more controlling approach may be needed in situations where competence or reliability are in question – an overly 'permissive' approach could be just as damaging as an overly 'authoritarian' approach – but if people are to change they need scope to be able to do new things. People cannot change if they feel completely disempowered.

DIMENSIONS OF DIFFERENCE

Apart from 'drivers' and other such personality traits, there are many other ways in which supervisors and supervisees may be different or alike: many different dimensions of difference. Supervisor or supervisee may have similar or different theoretical orientations, for instance. (*Everyone* has a theoretical orientation, including people who aren't aware of using any particular formal theory, and including people who are scornful of theory.) They may be similar or different ages, the same or different genders. They may have similar or different personal circumstances, and similar or different personal histories.

Importantly too, they may have the same or different cultural backgrounds, using 'culture' here in the broadest sense to refer to any particular set of ideas, manners, customs and beliefs that people have internalised over their lifetime from their surroundings. Hawkins and Shohet (2012: 113), drawing on Herskovits (1948), define culture as the 'explicit and implicit assumptions and values that influence the behaviour and social artefacts of different groups'.

A supervisor from a middle-class background, for instance, is likely to have different cultural assumptions from a supervisee from a working-class background, and a different perspective on the lives of service users. When supervisor and supervisee come from different parts of the world, or are members of different ethnic groups with origins in different parts of the world, they are likely to come to supervision with different assumptions about a wide range of topics. Hawkins and Shohet (2012: 115, drawing on a variety of sources) list fifteen different variables that may be involved in cultural differences. These include:

- Time management approaches
- Self-disclosure (for instance, in some cultures, it may be bad manners to ask people about how much money they earn, in other cultures it may be considered intrusive to ask people about what kind of childhood they had)

- Equality versus hierarchy (i.e. in some cultures it is less acceptable to challenge people in authority than it is in others)
- Outer directed versus inner directed (for instance, introspection and self-criticism may be more normal in some cultures than others).

They also note two dimensions identified by Ryde (1997):

- A continuum between the valuing of the experience of individuals and the valuing of the group
- A continuum between emotional expressiveness and emotional restraint.

Since our starting point in this chapter was *power*, we need to remember that the many possible differences between supervisor and supervisee will include combinations in which one half of the supervision dyad experiences itself as having more power in society generally than the other does. For instance, one thing that has struck me very much over my years of teaching social work students, is that way in which male students in a class are able or feel enabled to be more vocal than female students, even if in a minority in terms of numbers in a class. Research supports this observation (see, for instance, Nittrouer et al., 2018). (Of course there are highly vocal female students and very quiet male students, since other factors such as class and race also come into play and none of us is simply a representative of whatever demographic category we happen to belong to.) The prejudices and privileges in society play out in supervision sessions too.

EXERCISE 4.4

Differences and similarities between supervisors and supervisees

We have discussed various dimensions of difference, including gender, ethnicity, national origin, age, and social class. (These are examples of 'social divisions' [Payne, 2013]. Other social divisions I could have mentioned would have been gay/straight, disability, religious allegiance, etc.) I will now suggest various combinations of people who differ in respect of one or more social division, who might come together in supervision:

- Young woman + middle-aged man
- Young man + middle-aged woman
- Young woman from an African country + middle-aged white woman born in Britain

- Middle-aged Black British man with working-class background + middle-aged white man with middle-class background
- Young woman with white working-class background + middle-aged woman with white middle-class background
- Young woman with Black British working-class background + middle-aged white man with middle-class background
- Young white man with middle-class background + middle-aged Black British woman with working-class background

Clearly you cannot know how these differences would play out in supervision without also knowing about the personalities, drivers and personal histories of the individuals involved, and it would be wrong to make generalisations. However, drawing on your own personal experience, and on the experience of others you know, I would like you to ask yourself how these differences might affect the quality of the supervisory experience (a) if the first person in each pair was the supervisor and the second person was the supervisee, and (b) if it was the other way round, and the second person was the supervisor and the first person was the supervisee. (Feel free to explore this with combinations not listed above if more relevant to your experience.)

Then I would like you to review you own experiences of supervision (either as supervisee, or as supervisor, or both) and consider the combinations you have personally experienced and what you have learned from them.

In each example there are power differences along different dimensions. If we consider the pairings White/Black, Male/Female, Middle-class/Working-class, Middle-aged/Young, in each case the first category in the pair has more power in society than the second category. That this is true in the case of Male/Female is illustrated, for instance by my example of male students feeling more able to speak out than female students. (In reality of course, these different dimensions are typically in play at the same time, interacting to create more complicated scenarios, which is what is meant by the term 'intersectionality' [coined by Kimberle Crenshaw, 1989]). This means that, of the two people in supervision, one may belong to a group with more power in society than the other. If that person is also the supervisor then this may add to the legitimate power that this person already possesses by virtue of her/his role. On the other hand if the person from the more powerful group is the supervisee, then this may serve to detract from the legitimate power of the supervisor, who may then need to work harder to establish her authority. (In the final example above, the situation is more complicated because both participants belong to more or less powerful groups depending on which social division one considers.)

The degree to which power is added or subtracted in this way in practice will depend on the individual circumstances, but among the factors will be cultural ones.

For example, a young adult from a culture which places great emphasis on deference to age may find it particularly hard to challenge a considerably older adult.

As a general rule, differences (whether differences of gender, culture, age, ethnicity, personal circumstances or whatever else) between the supervisor and supervisee are beneficial to a supervision session because one of the purposes of supervision is to allow for several different perspectives to be brought to bear on the same problem (a form of triangulation). But the extent to which they are beneficial in practice must depend in part on (a) the willingness of the two parties to recognise and compare their different perspectives (as opposed to one deferring to the other, or one insisting on her own point of view as being simply 'correct') and (b) self-awareness on both sides of different senses of entitlement to power which each one brings to the session. It should not be the case, for instance, that a young female supervisor should feel that she 'ought not' to challenge a middle-aged male supervisee, or that a middle-aged male supervisor should act in a way that makes it difficult for a young female supervisee to express her own point of view.

EXERCISE 4.5

Power and difference overview

Consider one or more of the supervisory relationships you are currently involved in (or have been involved in), either as supervisor or supervisee. For each one, write down answers for the following questions:

- How successful a supervisory relationship it is/was and what are its strengths and weaknesses.
- The degree to which the supervisor was/is able to exercise legitimate power.
- Other kinds of power possessed by each participant.
- What seem to be the drivers of both parties – are they the same or different? – and the effect of these on the supervisory relationship.
- Differences and similarities between the two parties in terms of age, social class, ethnicity, country of origin, gender … and any other social division which is relevant.
- What does supervision help with in this particular pairing, and what does it fail to help with? What could you do to make it more helpful? (This may of course involve asking the other participant to do something different.)
- If you are a supervisor, what kind of supervisor do YOU become with this supervisee, and how does it differ from how you are with other supervisees? If you are a supervisee, what kind of supervisee do you become? In both cases, is it a good thing that you become like this, or is it something you should resist?

CONCLUDING NOTES FOR SUPERVISORS AND SUPERVISEES

Notes for supervisors (including practice educators)

Exercising authority over other people is difficult to get right, but it is important to own and use the authority that comes with the job of supervisor. Previous experience of learning to own the authority of being a professional practitioner should help. In both cases, an honest appraisal of your own relationship with power is a valuable exercise. Chapter 7 may assist with this because it will look, among other things, at different 'games' that supervisors play depending on their feelings about power. You may recognise yourself in some of them.

Important to get hold of, I suggest, is that 'care' and 'control' (see also 'responsiveness'/'demandingness' or 'task orientation/'people orientation') are not opposites but are separate dimensions. Just because you are getting the supportiveness right in the supervisory relationship doesn't mean you don't still have work to do on getting the challengingness right, and vice versa. Understanding your own drivers helps you to recognise which aspects of the task you may find harder and may be keener to avoid.

But thinking of yourself as being a particular kind of supervisor may be a simplification because the kind of supervisor you are may vary depending on which supervisee you are dealing with. It is of course entirely appropriate to adjust your supervision style to meet the needs of different supervisees, but it is worth considering whether this is in fact what you are doing, or whether certain kinds of supervision just become easier or more difficult depending on the supervisee.

While of course closer oversight is appropriate where there is reason to question the competence or commitment of a supervisee, it is important to remember too that, if you want someone to change, you also have to allow them to change. (This is true also of work with involuntary service users.) This means that in some way you need to empower them.

Notes for supervisees (including students on placement)

The supervisor/supervisee relationship is a professional one as well as a managerial one. The legitimate authority of the supervisor is important, but your own authority as a professional is also important. You should be able to express your thoughts on a case, and to discuss your feelings and intuitions. You should also be able to ask for specific things in supervision. For instance: 'I'm confused about the X case. I would really value an opportunity to go over it in detail and get my thoughts in order.' But of course this does not mean you are free to ignore decisions made in supervision, or instructions given to you by your supervisor as your manager.

(Continued)

Supervisors are human. They have insecurities just as you do. You will not get the best out of supervision if you make your supervisor feel undermined. Apart from anything else, supervision is an important safety net. The fact that you answer to your supervisor means that your supervisor shares responsibility for your work.

Sometimes supervisors may abuse or misuse their power. This varies from trivial instances, such as the supervisor not giving you enough time to express your own thoughts, which you may be able to talk through in the supervision session itself, to more serious ones, such as your supervisor demanding more of you than you should reasonably be expected to take on, which you may be able to resolve in supervision but may need to take up with more senior managers.

CHAPTER SUMMARY

This chapter has looked at power and authority, and the way that they play out in the context of supervisor/supervisee relationships. It began by looking at different kinds of power which not only the supervisor but the supervisee may bring to supervision.

It then moved on to look at 'authoritativeness', drawing on Baumrind's parenting model to identify two distinct dimensions that are present, not only in parent–child relationships, but in all kinds of relationships where one party has responsibility for the other (teacher/pupil, social worker/service user ... etc.): 'responsiveness' and 'demandingness'. I discussed why different supervisors might be more comfortable with being 'demanding' or being 'responsive'.

This led into a discussion of the different 'drivers' or 'scripts' that each of us brings to our relationships. Expressed in the form 'I'll be OK if ...' these scripts describe things we feel we need to do in order to be acceptable to others. I explored the effect of different drivers on supervision style, and considered how the drivers of supervisor and supervisee might interact.

I discussed the way that perceptions of the competence and reliability of supervisees (or indeed of supervisors) will also have a bearing on the supervisory relationship and touched on the risk of an overly controlling response, referring to the 'set-up-to-fail syndrome'.

I looked at other 'dimensions of difference', including age, social class, gender and ethnicity, which will also have an effect on the nature of the supervisory relationship, and may either reinforce or undercut the power of the supervisor.

5

CASEWORK AT SECOND HAND

CONTENTS

In this chapter, we return to the supervisory cycle, which is to say, the process by which decisions and action plans emerge in supervision from the material that the supervisee brings to it. In Chapter 2, I introduced the 4-element model of this cycle introduced by Jane Wonnacott and Tony Morrison (Wonnacott, 2012). What this chapter will focus on is the earlier half of the cycle, the two 'elements' that in Wonnacott's terminology are called 'Experience' and 'Reflection'. (Again, I remind the reader that these terms are used in a much narrower sense than their everyday meaning.) My starting point is a problem that all supervisors face:

1 Work they are responsible for, and could be held accountable for were anything to go wrong, largely takes place out of their sight, with people who they have often never met.
2 In trying to determine whether a good enough job has been done by their supervisees, they are largely reliant on information provided by the supervisees themselves.

THE PROBLEM OF NOT BEING THERE

A family has been reported to Children's Social Care by a neighbour who would not give his name but claimed that the child in a family across the street – a boy aged nearly 4 called Daniel – was being daily subjected to verbal abuse by his mother's partner, Mike. The neighbour alleged that Mike can be heard yelling at Daniel every evening, with Daniel crying and sometimes screaming in fear. The neighbour also suspects physical abuse, and says that Daniel sometimes has bruises on the backs of his legs like he's been slapped hard. The neighbour says that Mike is a big powerful man, a former parachute regiment sergeant, who does not like to be crossed, while Daniel's mother, Susan, is very quiet and never seems to question her husband. The neighbour also claimed to have heard at second hand from other neighbours who were once friendly with the family, that Daniel's room is very bare, with no toys, and only a mattress on the floor. Agency checks have been done. The family are not known to other professionals in the area (Daniel is not yet at school), so there is very little else to go on, but the neighbour was sufficiently concerned, and sufficiently convincing to the social worker who took the call, for the manager of the relevant team to decide that an exploratory visit is needed, and to send a social worker out, although she does not think a formal child protection investigation is warranted at this stage.

The social worker who goes out is a man called Godfrey. He is 26 years old and single with no children. You are his supervisor and he has been working in your team since he qualified three years ago.

On his return Godfrey reports that he feels quite satisfied that the referral was malicious. Mike, who is 35, was not the little boy's father, but had been living with Daniel's mother since Daniel was six months old. (The father's whereabouts are not known.) Mike had been very reasonable about the visit under the circumstances, assuring Godfrey that he perfectly understood that Godfrey was only doing his job. Godfrey says that when he described the neighbour's allegations, Mike had laughed loudly, and said that he could see how this might arise, because he does have a very loud voice – Godfrey confirms that this is the case – and is prone to bellow a bit, but he means no harm, and Daniel knows this. Godfrey says that Mike told him that he and Daniel have been playing a game recently where he pretends to be a monster chasing after Daniel, and shouting things like 'I'm coming to get you, you horrible little boy', and Daniel runs screaming until Mike catches him and gives him a tickle. It's all in fun, Mike assured Godfrey, and Daniel loves it, begging him to play, and shrieking with delight when he does.

'I can see how that might be misunderstood, actually,' said Mike, according to Godfrey. 'But you can see for yourself that everything's fine.' Godfrey says that Mike added that there had been 'a little bit of a disagreement lately' with one of the neighbours who seemed to think that he owned exclusive parking rights to the space in front of his house. 'They're the type that have been here forever, and resent newcomers like us until we've been here long enough to be accepted,' Mike observed. 'They're probably alright really, but they were totally out of order with this parking thing, and threatened us with trouble if we ever parked there again.'

Godfrey says that Susan, the mother, was quite quiet, but she seemed friendly and pleasant and she entirely backed up Mike's story. Godfrey says he also spoke to Daniel on his own. He seemed a perfectly cheerful little boy, if rather shy, and didn't seem to him to be at all intimidated by his father. Daniel had also confirmed the story about the noisy games of chase, and there was no sign of bruising on his legs. The house was comfortable and in 'beautiful condition' according to Godfrey. He had looked at Daniel's bedroom. It was pretty bare, but it did have a bed, and Mike had explained that they were about to redecorate it. He had shown Godfrey boxes of toys and clothes stored in the spare room.

As Godfrey tells it there is no cause for concern, and the case can now safely be closed.

As Godfrey's supervisor, you have a choice. You can decide that you agree with his judgement, or you can decide that more work is needed and ask Godfrey, or another member of your team, to do it. Your decision will depend on whether or not you feel that Godfrey has adequately explored the possible risk factors. But you have never met Daniel, or Mike, or Susan, and you only have Godfrey's account to tell you what they said, what they looked like, what frame of mind they seemed to be in, and what their home was like. Almost everything you know about the case is filtered through Godfrey. And, of course, Godfrey cannot give you a verbatim account of what was said: he can't remember the visit with that degree of detail. What he is telling you about are things he noted at the time, and certain judgements he made about what he saw and experienced. You might have shared his view if you'd been there, but then again, you might not have done.

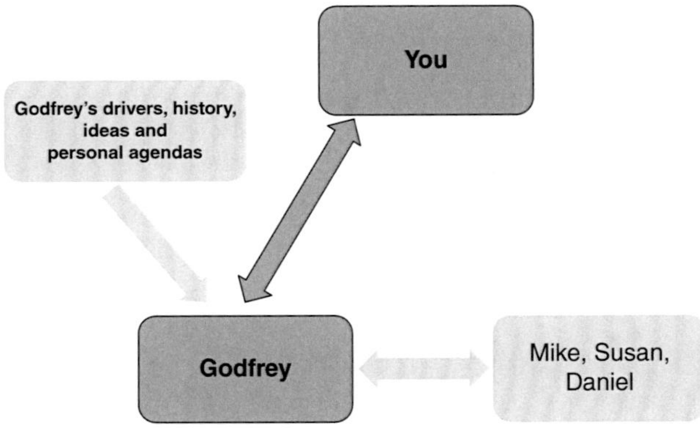

Figure 5.1 Things supervisors can see, and things they can't

Figure 5.1 sums up the situation. The things you as a supervisor can actually *see* are represented by the dark shapes: you, Godfrey and the interaction going on between the two of you. The pale, more ghostly shapes, represent things that you can't directly see, and only know through Godfrey's account of them. These include, of course, Daniel, Susan and Mike, and Godfrey's interaction with the three of them, but they also include Godfrey's history, his drivers, his ideas, his personal agendas, which you cannot have direct access to, but can only infer over time from getting to know him. Godfrey can't give you a word by word account of what was said in that visit, let alone provide you with an exact representation of the facial expressions, tones of voice, and body language used by the family (without which even a verbatim account would leave you with a lot of guesswork as to what was meant). What he tells you is limited by what he noticed, what he remembers, and what he thinks he *ought* to tell you. And all of those things – what he sees, notices, remembers and feels he ought to tell you – will be affected by those *other* things you can't see: Geoffrey's history, drivers, ideas and personal agendas.

To illustrate this problem another way, Figure 5.2 represents everything that's going on in that family for Daniel by the oval shape (A) and represents what Godfrey thinks he's learned by a smaller oval (B). This smaller oval crosses the edge of the larger one, because Godfrey's impressions include things that are really going on for Daniel, but since Godfrey's impressions inevitably involve some guesswork and inference, they are unlikely to correspond fully with the reality.

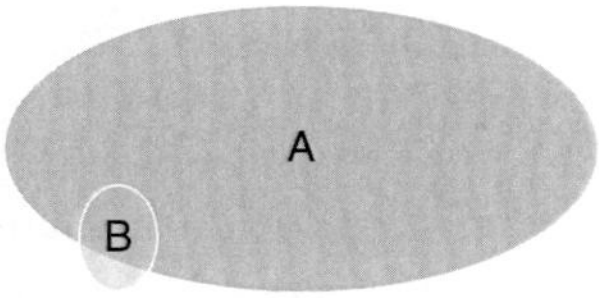

Figure 5.2 Daniel's world and what Godfrey understands of it

Your own impression of what is going on relies heavily on Godfrey's account, but you will give your own weighting to the things that Godfrey tells you, and what Godfrey tells you will itself depend to some extent on the questions you ask and how you ask them. Both the questions you ask and the way you *interpret* Godfrey's answers will be shaped by something you *do* have direct access to but don't necessarily notice because of its sheer familiarity: your own ideas, your own drivers, your history, your personal agenda. So I will represent what you understand about Daniel's circumstances by another oval, C, in Figure 5.3.

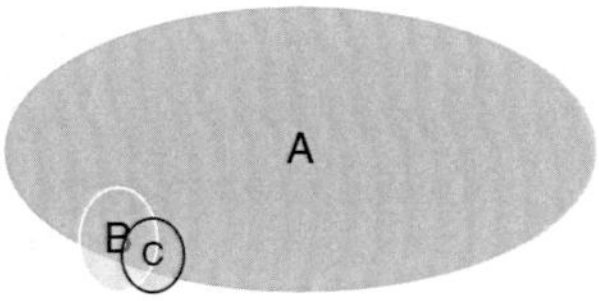

Figure 5.3 Daniel's world and what Godfrey's supervisor understands of it

C includes four segments. Figure 5.4, below, magnifies C to make this more clear. What you see of Daniel's experience is largely based on Godfrey's account and so will include (1) things going on that Godfrey correctly recognised and (2) things that he incorrectly inferred were going on. You know Godfrey to some extent and you are experienced in working with families, so you will make inferences of your own, some of which are accurate (3), some not (4).

As a supervisor, I would often form what felt like quite a coherent mental picture of a family that one of my supervisees was working with, but when I met the family, it would often turn out that the picture in my mind was wrong.

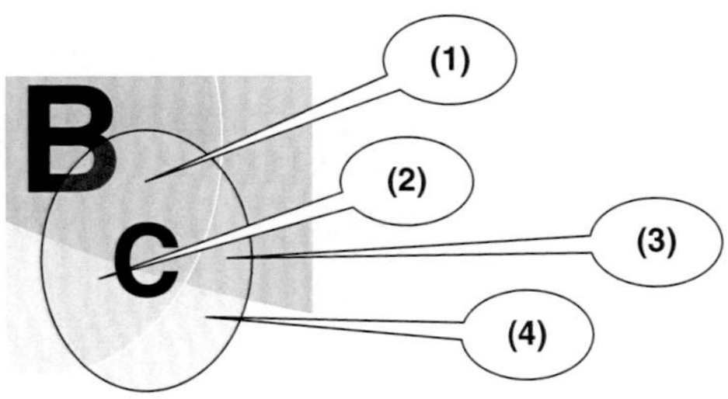

Figure 5.4 What Godfrey's supervisor understands of Daniel's world, close up

SEEING, REMEMBERING, TELLING

You may feel I am exaggerating the difficulties here. I would prefer to say that I am highlighting them. But it is true that the extent to which this problem is a serious one will depend on the situation. Sometimes the information needed to make a decision is fairly simple and straightforward, in which case the likelihood that a seriously inaccurate picture will be presented in supervision is not so great. But in a situation like the one in the example, the problem is very real, for the question to be answered is whether there is any reason to think that Daniel may be at risk of serious harm, and there is no straightforward way of measuring this. Coming to a reasonable judgement on the risks depends on getting an accurate sense of the relationships within the family. Without rigorous supervision, the likelihood of getting an accurate picture is likely to be reduced.

To illustrate this, suppose that you, as a supervisor, were to ask Godfrey simply to sum up for you what he learned on the visit. There are a number of different factors that will influence the account he gives you.

1 *Noticing and not noticing*. Godfrey noticed some things. Of the things he noticed, some he may have noticed but then pushed out of his mind. Some things he simply didn't notice.
2 *Remembering and forgetting*. Of the things he noticed and did not push out of his mind, he remembers some things, though not always accurately.
3 *Weighting*. Out of the things he still remembers, some things will seem important to him, others not. If you simply invite him to give you his own account, naturally he will focus on what seems to him important.
4 *Interpretation*. He will probably have come to some sort of conclusion about the visit (that is on whether Daniel is at risk and whether any kind of follow-up is required), based on the things that he can remember and that seem to him important. If he has reached such a conclusion, he is likely to tell the story in a way that leads naturally to this conclusion.
5 *Preferred outcome*. There will be things that he wants you to say, and things that he would rather you didn't say, about what should happen next. Most people in supervision tend, at least to some extent, to present their material in a way that favours their desired outcome. (That is: they present it in a way that is more likely to get their supervisor to come to the conclusion they want her to reach – a bit like a lawyer presenting a case in a courtroom.) I would suggest that all or some of the previous four stages may also be influenced by Godfrey's desired outcome. That is: what he notices or fails to notice, what he remembers or forgets, what he decides is important, and what interpretation he chooses to make – all of these may to some extent be influenced by what he wants to happen next.

Part of the job of a supervision session is to disrupt this human tendency to construct a story that suits us. So, rather than asking Godfrey to tell you what he noticed or what he remembered, you might prefer to ask specific questions: 'How would you describe Susan?' 'How much time did you spend with Daniel on his own?' 'What precisely was in Daniel's bedroom?' etc. This may yield information which Godfrey had forgotten about. It may reveal gaps in what he noticed: things that one might have expected him to notice but which for some reason he didn't (which itself can be revealing). You may also notice emotional responses: things that seem to make him feel uncomfortable, things that he doesn't seem to want to talk about. And, by asking your own questions rather than just listening, you break up the account which he has constructed in his mind and allow both him and you to consider the possibility that there might be other ways of describing what he saw.

Psychologists speak of 'confirmation bias', meaning that, 'contrary to the rules of philosophers of science, who advise testing hypotheses by trying to refute them, people ... seek data that are likely to be compatible with the beliefs they currently hold' (Kahneman, 2011: 81). The illusionist Derren Brown has built his whole career on persuading audiences that X is going on, so that they fail to notice that what is actually happening is Y, and he does this by making use of confirmation bias: 'We are not dispassionate judges when we have a belief, however tenuous, already in place,' he writes. 'To look at things objectively and step outside our beliefs is almost impossible' (Brown, 2007: 276–7). But, if your supervision with Godfrey is to add any value to his assessment, and not simply rubber-stamp what he has already concluded, you need to challenge that bias, by behaving like the awkward audience member at a magic show, who refuses to look where the magician wants her to look. To do this you need to ask questions that may not have occurred to him, interrogate the inferences he has made, and invite him to look for alternative interpretations to the ones he's come with by himself.

By challenging supervisees to notice and remember things they might otherwise not notice or might forget, a supervisor is also training them to notice and remember more on future occasions.

One thing in particular supervisors can encourage supervisees to do is notice their feelings.

FEELINGS AND DEFENCES

Professionals should be dispassionate and objective, yes? They should disregard their own personal feelings and concentrate on the facts.

There is *some* truth in these statements. Acting professionally does mean doing the right thing, regardless of our own personal feelings. But, as I have already briefly discussed in Chapter 2, this doesn't mean that someone like Godfrey should ignore his feelings when visiting Daniel's family, or that to have feelings, or to pay attention to them is in some way unprofessional. Godfrey may *think* that his feelings are irrelevant, and try to disregard them. He may be a little ashamed of some of his feelings (our feelings towards service users are not always positive ones). Or he may pay them no attention, and, unless he is asked, not even mention them in supervision. But paying attention to his feelings is actually vitally important if he and his supervisor are to get a sense of what was going on during his visit. As Richard Ingram observes, 'emotions are inextricably linked to social work decision making' (2013: 17) – and the same is true of any kind of professional decision-making involving human situations because our feelings influence what we notice and how we interpret what we notice.

There are several reasons for this:

Gut feelings

Feelings exist for a reason. They constitute a kind of rough assessment of a situation which can be the basis for immediate action. A zebra sees a large object apparently creeping towards it through the grass, it feels instant fear, and it bolts ... A man approaches you and you feel there is something fake about his apparent friendliness, so you instantly put yourself on alert against the possibility that he intends you harm ... These instant emotional reactions often turn out to be wrong – the object creeping through the grass may just be an empty plastic bag blowing in the wind – but they're extremely useful. If the zebra were to decide to ignore its fear reaction to objects creeping towards it, it will end up being eaten sooner rather than later.

Psychologists talk about two distinct systems in the mind:

- *System 1* operates automatically and quickly, with little or no effort and no sense of voluntary control.
- *System 2* allocates attention to the effortful mental activities that demand it, including complex computations. The operations of System 2 are often associated with the subjective experience of agency, choice, and concentration. (Kahneman, 2011: 20–1)

The zebra's panic reaction is an example of System 1 in operation. On the other hand, if an observer were to decide to examine slowed down video footage of the scene in order to identify the large object in the grass, that would be an example of System 2 in operation. System 1 can be a life-saver when there is no time for thinking, but it is an unconscious response to a few stimuli (in the zebra's case: 'here is a large unidentified object which reminds me of predators'), and the picture of the world it offers often needs modifying in the light of more detailed information, meaning that an instant reaction should be avoided if possible. Perhaps the friendliness of the man in the street only seems fake to you because he reminds you a bit of an unpleasant person you used to know? You might realise his friendliness was completely genuine if you knew him better.

Unless you are in a situation where there is quite literally no time to think, it is important not to take one's initial 'System 1' response as necessarily being an accurate picture of what is going on. But that doesn't mean we should disregard it. People sometimes say of someone they meet, 'I don't know why but X gives me the creeps' (by which I suppose they mean something like 'X's friendliness is fake in some way and I sense another agenda – perhaps an abusive one – beneath the surface'). This gut feeling is not in itself evidence of wrong doing or bad intentions on X's part, of course, but it would be foolish to ignore it completely because it represents an unconscious distillation of a lifetime's experience. Perhaps we find X creepy because he reminds us of other people whose motives we had good reason to distrust, and we have recognised something in X's demeanour that indicates an unpleasant agenda beneath the surface? This might be wrong. It may mean no more than we had once a bad experience with someone whose hair colour was the same as X's. But if the gut feeling is a persistent one, and particularly if it is shared by several people, it would be foolish to ignore it. It is not hard evidence in itself – you can't take someone to court for seeming creepy – but it is an indication that it would be a good idea to dig deeper.

The enquiry report into the death of 6-year-old Rikki Neave in Peterborough in 1997 noted that the social workers who visited felt extremely intimidated by Rikki's mother, Ruth (who was subsequently found guilty of child cruelty) and made the point that this fear was, in itself, *information*. If these adults were frightened by this woman, how might a 6-year-old child feel? (Bridge Consultancy, 1997).

Empathy

'Mrs Brown just seemed so frightened and alone sitting there in her wheelchair with her grown-up kids all round her arguing about what we should do with her,' says a community nurse, returning after a visit to a physically frail elderly woman, most of whose children feel she should be in residential care. Attunement to the feelings of vulnerable service users is important. After all, the aim of all human services is to improve the quality of people's lives, and quality of life is very much a matter of how we *feel*.

But intuiting the feelings of others involves being in touch with our own feelings. If we decided it was unprofessional even to notice our own feelings, we would miss out on this insight into the feelings of others.

Subjectivity

But our emotional responses to situations are the product, not just of the situation, but of our own mental states. When we are feeling depressed, for instance, the world looks darker and we are more prone to see evidence of darkness.

We also tend to respond to aspects of a situation that we feel we recognise from our own experience. If you are a woman recovering from a painful breakup with a cheating male partner, you may be more prone to suspect men in general of being cheats, or to assume that men are the 'bad guys' in the relationships which you encounter in your work. If you gave up several years of your life to looking after a much-loved parent, you may find yourself feeling angry with a son who wants to put his parent in a home, even though you have no knowledge of their relationship and no reason to think that it is the same as your relationship with your own parent.

Sometimes too, social workers have feelings about service users personally which are not relevant to the case, but which are likely to colour their view. We can feel angry with service users who do not find our services helpful. We can feel gratitude towards service users who appreciate us. We may find some service users intimidating for reasons that are irrelevant to the case (as well as for reasons that do tell us a lot about the case, as in the Neave case discussed above). We may be very drawn to particular service users. All of these are feelings we are bound to have sometimes, and having them is not in itself unprofessional. What would be unprofessional would be to refuse to admit to ourselves that we had those feelings, and then allow our practice to be influenced by them anyway. For example: if we avoid visiting someone who makes us doubt ourselves, but actually has quite serious problems, and then go and lavish time and effort on someone who makes us feel good, but whose needs are nothing like as great, that would be unprofessional.

As an additional layer of complication, there may also be a cultural component to our feelings. We may be more suspicious of people whose cultural practices are different from our own. Each culture has its own ideas about personal space, for instance, meaning that a person from another culture may seem either aloof or intrusive (or even creepy) when in fact they are just behaving in the way that is normal for them. And we should also not rule out the possibility that our perceptions may be affected by prejudices of one kind or another: possibly prejudices which we ourselves are not aware of. Several studies have shown, for instance, that white people are more likely to feel that a Black person was behaving in a threatening or dangerous way than they would if a white person was doing exactly the same thing (Plant and Peruche, 2005; Brooker and Repper, 2009). This may be the case, even if the white people concerned are not consciously aware of having such a prejudice.

For all these reasons our feelings about a situation cannot be taken as an accurate representation of what is really happening. We have to understand ourselves a bit in order to be able to disentangle our own histories from the situation in front of us. Supervision can help with this but, for that to happen, it needs to be an environment within which it is acceptable for supervisees to discuss feelings, and to consider what they mean. For if feelings are *not* considered, they don't disappear. They are still there, influencing how we see the world. It is just that both supervisee and supervisor will be unaware, or less aware, of their influence. Feelings are a bit like tinted lenses that colour the image that's seen through them. It is in the supervisor's interest to understand what kind of lenses their supervisees are looking through.

Psychological defences

I mentioned above that what we notice or remember may be influenced by what we want to happen. To illustrate what I mean by that, here is an example from my own experience. Many years ago when I was still a social work practitioner, I had on my caseload a family which was dominated by an extremely powerful and highly controlling mother, whose behaviour was thought to be, or certainly to border on, emotional abuse, with some concerns about physical abuse as well. Her children were clearly intimidated by her and so, if I'm honest, was I. One time, after a difficult and lengthy visit (I no longer remember what it was about), I was leaving just as the youngest child came home from somewhere and, as I met this child in the hallway, I noticed he had a bruise on his face. I no longer remember what sort of bruise it was (these events occurred 30 years ago), but what I do still remember is that there was a moment in which I almost decided to tell myself that I hadn't seen it. I found it very uncomfortable being in that house, I had been there for a long time, and I really didn't want to have to spend any more time there. In this case, I spotted the self-deception. I made myself notice the bruise and ask the boy and his parents how it had occurred. But the incident made me wonder afterwards how many other things, perhaps more subtle things than bruises, I might have managed not to notice in the course of my career without even being aware of what I was up to?

Whether or not you buy into psychodynamic psychology as a whole package, the idea of psychological defences, once you get hold of it, makes sense, and the various defences identified by Freud and others can easily be spotted going on around you. Many of us for instance have experienced at first or second hand the phenomenon of going into 'denial' on receiving news that is simply too shocking to process all at once. *Denial* is a way of protecting ourselves by simply refusing to accept the reality of a distressing event. Another defence mechanism is *displacement*, where we shift 'the focus of attention from an object that is unacceptable to a safer one' (Bowins, 2004: 9): this may be going on when human service professionals busy themselves with procedures, meetings and IT systems as a way of avoiding having to directly face the suffering of their patients or clients. *Reaction formation* 'reduces the conscious perception of unacceptable impulses by transforming them into their opposite' (Bowins, 2004: 11–12), as might occur if we found ourselves fearing someone, but, in order to avoid acknowledging that fact, we told ourselves that we really liked them. *Projection* 'facilitates the perception that disturbing impulses and ideas arise from outside the self' (Bowins, 2004: 11) by allowing us to attribute them to other people, as might happen if a supervisee, unable to face her own anger with a client, attributed it to the client herself.

We can all identify these kinds of manoeuvres, if we are honest with ourselves. In fields such as social work or nursing, which deal with highly distressing subject matter (abuse, disability, loss, death ...) and often with very distressed or angry people, it would be surprising if such defence mechanisms did not influence what is noticed by practitioners and how it is interpreted.

Countertransference

The term 'countertransference' is used in a number of different ways (discussed by Gibbons et al., 2011), but it refers to the way a psychotherapist or similar professional may become emotionally over-involved with a client, either as a response to the client's 'transference' (the client's projection of feelings from her past onto the therapist), or because the therapist projects feelings from *her* past onto the client. It is this second sense that I want to draw your attention to here. (If you dislike the Freudian trappings, you could just call it 'over-involvement' or 'over-identification'.)

The simplest explanation I have come across of how countertransference can play out in the helping professions is provided by a paper by Alan Carr (1989) who discussed the kinds of countertransference that can occur in a professional team when working with families where there has been child abuse. (The paper is freely available online, and I recommend reading it in full, though some of the language is a little old-fashioned.) What Carr notices is that countertransference often occurs in this kind of work, and that it takes a number of forms. He classifies these using Karpman's 'Drama Triangle' (1968). The Triangle refers to the way in which people reduce human situations in which they are involved into a simplified fairytale-like drama containing just three stereotypical roles – Victim, Persecutor and Rescuer – and Carr proposes five countertransference reactions (CTRs) that he distinguishes from one another on the basis of who is assigned to each of these roles. One of these five he calls *Rescuing the child*:

> Here the worker in the position of rescuer, views the abused child as a victim of the persecuting parents and all who advocate on their behalf ... [This CTR] is characterized by an intense emotional desire to protect the child. It may be accompanied by an additional desire to persecute the parents. The child is

> experienced as someone who would gladly be forever separated from the parents. The parents are experienced as … undeserving of the child. Evidence which points to parental competence and the child's desire to be with the parents is minimized, denied or discounted … Workers with this CTR become involved in angry disagreements with team members who point to factors which suggest that family rehabilitation is possible. (Carr, 1989: 89)

This is not to say that a worker who feels that a child should not be returned to an abusive parent is necessarily in the grip of a CTR. Sometimes this is an entirely reasonable conclusion to come to. What makes this a CTR is the rigidity of the worker who has succumbed to it, their unwillingness to even consider alternative points of view, and their refusal to look at evidence which is inconsistent with their views. I suspect that many people in the child care field will have experienced themselves or others being in the grip of that kind of completely inflexible conviction. Workers in the adult field have told me they see similar patterns in relation to primary clients and their carers.

By calling this phenomenon a countertransference reaction, Carr is suggesting that the power and rigidity of the worker's conviction comes from the fact that the worker is identifying the family with people from her own past, perhaps a previous family she worked with where she failed to protect a child from harm, or even more powerfully (particularly in the case of younger workers) with her own family of origin. She has come to see the people in the current situation as characters from some past experience, and is now re-enacting that previous story.

Another common CTR is *Rescuing the parents*:

> When this CTR occurs, the worker, in the position of rescuer, construes the parents as victims of a hostile social environment and a punitive child protection system … [and] experiences a strong desire to support the parents and ensure that they retain custody of the abused child. An intense sense of outrage at social circumstances such as unemployment, poor housing or social isolation which places stress upon the parents is felt … Evidence which points to parental incompetence, and factors which suggest that the child is at risk when living with the parents is minimized, denied or discounted. Within the team, the worker may accuse colleagues of 'playing it safe' … [and] may become engaged in heated arguments where they [the worker] define current child protection laws and practices as an intrusive involvement of the state in family life. (Carr, 1989: 90–1)

Carr suggests that 'workers who have insecurities about their adequacy as parents and their capacity to meet their own children's need for nurturance and safety may be prone to experiencing this CTR' (1989: 91). I wonder whether workers may also be prone to it when their own parents were well-meaning but, for understandable reasons, such as poor mental health, were limited in the care and nurturing they could provide. Someone with that background may have grown up having to suppress their awareness of unmet need resulting from their parents' limitations, while telling themselves that their parents were good people and everything was fine.

Whether or not you 'buy' such historical explanations, the patterns themselves are readily observable. Indeed it is my experience that most social workers in the child care field are, to some extent, either 'child rescuers' or 'parent rescuers', even if not usually in these extreme forms, and with some fluctuation between one position and the other from case to case. ('Parent rescuers' are not people who are indifferent to the needs of the child, it's important to note, but they emphasise the child's need to be with her family of origin above other needs.) A supervisor needs to be aware of where her supervisees sit on that spectrum, and where she sits on it herself. One thing that can happen is that when several professionals are working with a family, and one of them experiences a CTR, another 'experiences a complementary CTR. For example, if one worker begins to rescue a child, another will try to rescue the parents. A similar process holds true for inter-agency working ... If CTRs remain outside awareness, such polarization will continue until inter-worker or inter-agency cooperation becomes impossible' (Carr, 1989: 95). Again, in my experience, this polarisation between agencies is a common pattern. I think, for instance, of cases where a mental health agency has taken a very rigid 'parent rescuer' position in relation to a parent with a mental health problem, while a child care agency has taken an equally rigid 'child rescuer' position.

Carr argues that CTRs cannot be avoided and can even be useful (a 'child rescuer' for instance, may be very attuned to what is missing for the child in a given situation, a 'parent rescuer' to what the parents need to have in order to be able to do a better job), but they do need to be brought into awareness. 'Once in awareness, valid information contained in various team members' CTRs may be distinguished from workers' personal contributions to CTR processes. This valid information may be usefully incorporated into the team's evaluation of the family being treated' (Carr, 1989: 95).

THE BACK STORY

'Valid information' in the quote above means genuine insights into the client's experience. 'Personal contributions' means material from the worker's own background that has become entangled in the worker's mind with the client's experience. What I have been trying to show is that, when the supervisee in a supervision session recounts the story of what has been happening in one of her cases, there is always a back story, a reason why the story is being told in *this particular way*. This may not be very important for the supervisor to know about if the information being reported is relatively simple and unambiguous, but in more complex situations, you need to have some sense of the back story to understand the story itself. I will illustrate this by returning to the story of Godfrey's visit to Daniel and his family, this time adding some material about Godfrey's experience that was not included in the earlier account:

> You are Godfrey. You are not very confident about your work, something you do your best to conceal, and often worry that you're simply not up to the demands of the job. You find it particularly difficult to deal with angry or threatening behaviour. You have a very strong tendency to want to please people, and your first instinct in tense situations is always to reassure or placate, even if this means overlooking aspects of the situation. Most of us do not fully understand our own drivers, and you do not fully understand these facts about yourself.
>
> You visited Daniel's family in some trepidation. These visits are always difficult and you anticipated having to deal with anger from Mike and Susan at the intrusion. In fact, and to your huge relief, Mike greeted you in a friendly way at the door, assured you that he perfectly understood that you had to investigate these things and that you were only doing your job. 'I couldn't do your job, mate.' This was actually rather flattering, given that he was a former paratrooper.
>
> The house was immaculate, very different from a lot of the houses you visit. Mike and Susan were both good-looking, smartly dressed people, Susan very petite, Mike a handsome man with a good deal of charm and a rugby-player's physique. Susan seemed quiet but not unfriendly, and offered you a cup of tea.
>
> Mike asked you why it was you were visiting, while Susan went and made the tea. (With hindsight, you know you should not have accepted the tea and should have asked her to remain in the conversation.) When you told Mike about the neighbour's allegations, he laughed and gave you the explanation you later reported to your supervisor about the whole thing having been a noisy game. You didn't really question him about it, you just noted his explanation and told him it sounded reasonable.
>
> You asked to see Daniel. He was a thin, quiet little boy who seemed quite frightened by the visit, but you reminded yourself that most kids would be. Mike and Susan left the room when you asked to see Daniel on his own ('Of course, if that's what you need to do!'), but the truth is you got almost nothing out of Daniel. He only gave monosyllabic answers to your questions, and you let him go after only a couple of minutes. He was wearing shorts and you didn't see any bruises on his legs, but you didn't specifically look for bruises.

When Mike showed you Daniel's bedroom, it did look bare and that worried you, but he gave you the explanation about how they planned to redecorate it and you accepted that gratefully without further questions. Then you left, apologising for any upset caused.

Out in the street you briefly noticed that your heart was racing, and that your hands were slippery with sweat. (You're not a very confident worker, it's true, but that doesn't normally happen after a visit!) If you had allowed yourself to think about it, you might perhaps have noticed that you found Mike terrifying and how the whole time you were there your whole attention, and all your energy, had been focused on keeping him as friendly and pleasant as he had been when he first answered the door. You might also have noticed how grateful you felt to Mike for not giving you a hard time. But you did not allow yourself to think about these things.

One thing is certain, though. You do not want to have to deal with, or think about this family ever again.

EXERCISE 5.1

Getting to Feelings

So we now have two accounts of Godfrey's visit to Daniel's family. The first account, at the beginning of the chapter, is what Godfrey reported back to his supervisor. The second account, above, tells you more about what the experience was actually like for Godfrey.

- If you were Godfrey's supervisor, how much would it alter your opinion about Geoffrey's original account, if you became aware of Godfrey's feelings during the visit, as just described?
- What might be the significance of his feelings?
- Why might Godfrey not discuss his reaction with you? Why, in general, might he not talk about his feelings in supervision?
- What might you, as his supervisor, do to encourage him to notice and share things like that?
- What sorts of questions might you ask in supervision in order to elicit this kind of material?

If I were Godfrey's supervisor, and I discovered just how intimidated Godfrey had been by Mike, it would raise serious doubts in my mind about the reliability and safety of his report. It now seems clear that he had been unable to focus on carrying out a risk assessment for Daniel because of his preoccupation with placating Mike and preventing Mike from being angry with him. Godfrey is also very keen not to have to go back there, so much so that it seems likely that he has presented the story (without deliberately being dishonest) in the way he thinks most likely to satisfy you that no further action is required.

Why did he have such a powerful emotional reaction? Given that, even for Godfrey, this strong reaction was atypical, it suggests to me that Mike has some special significance for Godfrey. Perhaps he reminded Godfrey of a frightening individual from his own childhood? If so, this is not to say that Godfrey was not picking up something real. If he has had a bad experience with an abusive adult in the past, he may actually be rather good at picking up the signs that someone is an abusive individual of a similar type.

On the other hand, perhaps those signs were pretty obvious. Perhaps any competent observer would have picked up that Mike's friendliness was a façade and that beneath the surface he was consumed by anger. It could be that the visceral fear that Godfrey felt was a pretty accurate reflection of what it felt like for Daniel, and perhaps Susan too, living in that house.

Perhaps a kind of *reaction formation* has taken place. Rather than face how frightening he found Mike, Godfrey has decided to tell himself that Mike was a friendly and understanding man who he really liked.

But then again, perhaps not. Perhaps Mike was indeed a good stepfather who happened to have a rather loud voice. You can't know which of these possibilities is correct without further exploration.

As to why Godfrey might not discuss his powerful emotional reaction in supervision (or indeed his feelings in general), there are a whole range of possibilities. One is that he might not take them seriously himself. On emerging from the house, he doubtless felt very relieved that he was out of there, but possibly a bit ashamed at how frightened he'd felt. Perhaps he just chalked the whole thing up to him being a bit of a wimp.

Even if he didn't dismiss his feelings like that, he might worry that if he talked about his feelings, his supervisor might think he was unsuitable for the job. Or he might think that his feelings were simply not relevant, just a private matter which there was no reason to burden his supervisor with. He might think that fear would be shameful to own up to, and tell himself he just needs to 'grow a pair'.

Supervisors can encourage their supervisees to take their feelings seriously in a number of different ways. At the beginning of the supervisory relationship, they can make clear that feelings are important and that supervisees should make a point of noting their feelings and feeling free to discuss them. They could even specifically ask supervisees to take note of their feelings during and after a piece of work.

They can also use a little self-disclosure – or make general observations about the emotional content of the work – to let the supervisee know that feelings like fear, anger or punitiveness are not at all unusual in this kind of work.

Questions you might ask as Godfrey's supervisor: 'What was your immediate feeling when Mike answered the door?' 'If you had to describe how Daniel made you feel when you first saw him, what would be the first word that sprang to mind?' 'When you came out of the house, what were your feelings?' 'I notice that when I asked you about X, you seemed to become very uneasy. Why was that?'

OTHER FEELINGS

In the example of Godfrey above, the dominant feeling seems to be fear. Fear is a pretty common emotion in human services generally, and one which it's important to allow for. In some cases the fear will be of actual physical violence, and in these cases it's obviously important that workers aren't expected to visit clients alone. But we may still dread someone's anger, even if we don't expect them to be violent. In the case of service users who aren't the least bit intimidating, we can still dread upsetting them, or disappointing them, or giving them a message that we know they won't want to hear. All these feelings have the potential to make us keen to avoid doing something that actually does need doing.

A rather different kind of fear (one might also call it horror) comes from exposure to material that most people would prefer not to think about, because it threatens our own feeling of security in the world. Most people do not want to think about the sexual abuse of children by adults, for instance, or about relationships in which one partner is controlled and dominated by the other through violence. Most people prefer not to think about death, illness, physical pain, psychotic illness or disability either. And while professionals of course become 'used' to dealing with such things, they don't do so without a cost, and they have to develop coping strategies. In her study of nurses, Isabel Menzies (aka Menzies Lyth), writes:

> Nurses are in constant contact with people who are physically ill or injured, often seriously. The recovery of patients is not certain and will not always be complete ... Nurses are confronted with the threat of death and suffering as few lay people are. Their work involves carrying out tasks which, by ordinary standards, are distasteful, disgusting, and frightening ... The work situation arouses very strong and mixed feelings in the nurse: pity, compassion and love; guilt and anxiety; hatred and resentment of the patients who arouse these strong feelings; envy of the care given the patient. (Menzies, 1960: 97–8)

She goes on to discuss a range of ways in which nurses cope with these feelings. One of these is *'Depersonalization, categorization and denial of the significance of the individual'* (1960: 101), an example of which is when a nurse, instead of referring to a patient by name, refers to them as '"the liver in bed 10" or "the pneumonia in bed 15"' (1960: 102). I suspect that anyone who works in a human service agency will be able to think of similar examples. Another defence is *'Detachment and denial of feelings'* (1960: 102), potentially very dangerous when (as discussed above) awareness of one's feelings may be essential to understanding what is going on. Another is *'The attempt to eliminate decisions by ritual task performance'* (1960: 103), something we see a *lot* in human service organisations. The important point to note here is that, not only our feelings themselves, but the various strategies we use to manage or distance ourselves from our feelings, affect our ability to understand what is going on in a situation.

Menzies mentioned anger towards patients. Anger or punitiveness can be hard to own up to but needs to be confronted if they are not to affect our judgements. Carr, in the paper cited above, speaks about how we can develop punitive feelings towards service users who will not let us help them:

> The ineffectiveness of the worker's interventions gives rise to a sense of impotence. The family is experienced as a persecutor who threatens the identity of the worker as a helping professional. Thus the worker experiences him or herself as a victim. (Carr, 1989: 94)

This probably applies in particular to workers who are not very confident in themselves as practitioners. But it is difficult to admit, even to oneself, that one feels persecuted by a vulnerable person that you are supposed to be trying to help. So, to draw such feelings out, it may be necessary for a supervisor to normalise such feelings by talking about the negative feelings helping professionals sometimes have towards their clients, or even by a little judicious self-disclosure.

Of course the opposite can happen when a service user is very grateful for your services, and says that no one has ever understood her like you do. This is likely to be a particularly powerful experience for a not very confident worker, because it provides in spades the reassurance and validation that the worker craves. It can lead to reciprocal gratitude, and even feelings of love and romantic attraction (a classic CTR!). Even if the feeling is not *that* strong it can skew practice because it tends to lead both to a desire to hold on to the case, and a resistance to noticing anything that might oblige us to behave in a way that the service user wouldn't like. A supervisor might spot that something of this kind is going on if her supervisee has cases which she is very reluctant to close, but also not particularly keen to discuss.

It is important to note that all the processes that can occur between client and professional can also happen between supervisee and supervisor. Supervisors too can feel punitive towards supervisees who don't seem to appreciate their help. Supervisors too can feel warm, grateful feelings towards supervisees who are very appreciative of their help, with the risk that they will begin to find it difficult to challenge the supervisee if this might risk the warmth of their relationship. And just as new practitioners, who are not yet very confident in themselves, are likely to be particularly vulnerable to such feelings, so are new supervisors.

GROUPTHINK

I previously mentioned groupthink in Chapter 3. You have experienced groupthink if you have ever found yourself in a group of people who all seem to agree on something and you decided you had better go along with the rest of them. It might happen with a group of friends talking about politics, or it might happen in a work context such as a case conference. You feel that there is a consensus, and you set aside your own views and doubts in order to conform to it. Perhaps your doubts remain but you choose not to speak them aloud – in my experience people who've been to a case conference often express private doubts afterwards that they didn't mention in the meeting – or perhaps you tell yourself that, if everyone else sees it that way, you must be wrong. But it's quite possible that many of the other people, or perhaps even *all* of them, have the same private doubts as you, so that the apparent consensus is completely illusory!

The term groupthink originates with the psychologist Irving Janis (1982) who looked at a number of famous disasters (the Bay of Pigs fiasco, the Cuban missile crisis, the Japanese attack on Pearl Harbor ...) and tried to understand how decisions were made. This led him to draw some general conclusions about the way groups seek consensus. I think these ideas are relevant to supervision because even two people constitute a kind of group, and groupthink can and does regularly occur even between just two individuals. Indeed, I would go as far as to say that the ordinary rules of politeness almost dictate a degree of groupthink, and much of the rest of this chapter could be seen as my encouragement to you to set aside in supervision the everyday convention in which, 'each party accepts the line put out by the other party ... what is said is accepted at its face value and "each participant is allowed to carry the role he has chosen for himself" unchallenged' (Kadushin, 1999 [1967]: 64, citing Goffman, 1967: 11).

The following are the symptoms of groupthink from Janis (1982: 174–5), with my own comments in italics:

Type I: Overestimation of the group – its power and morality

1 An illusion of invulnerability ... which creates excessive optimism ... [*I have seen this after a child protection conference, where the collective level of anxiety visibly drops when the group has made a decision, even though the decision might be wrong, and the actual day-to-day risk to the child may be largely unchanged. It can happen in a supervision session too, and in planning meetings, when both/all parties agree on a plan, and then reinforce each other's conviction that it is definitely the correct course of action, thereby reducing their anxiety.*]
2 An unquestioned belief in the group's inherent morality, inclining the group to ignore the ethical or moral consequences of their decisions [*This may be visible in disputes with other agencies, where it is assumed that 'they' must be in the wrong, because 'we' are manifestly in the right.*]

Type II: Close-mindedness

3 Collective efforts to rationalise in order to discount warnings or other information that might lead the members to reconsider their assumptions ... [*The concerns of someone outside the group might be discounted on the basis that they always worry about everything.*]
4 Stereotyped views of enemy leaders ... [*In a human service context, where there are no 'enemies', we might substitute 'other agencies with whom we disagree'.*]

Type III: Pressures toward uniformity

5 Self-censorship of deviations from the apparent group consensus, reflecting each member's inclination to minimize to himself the importance of his doubts and counterarguments
6 A shared illusion of unanimity concerning judgements conforming to the majority view (partly resulting from self-censorship of deviations, augmented by the false assumption that silence means consent)
7 Direct pressure on any member who expresses strong arguments against any of the group's stereotypes, illusions, or commitments, making clear that this type of consent is contrary to what is expected of all loyal members
8 The emergence of self-appointed mindguards – members who protect the group from adverse information that might shatter their shared complacency about the effectiveness and morality of their decisions.

What is being described here is a process that creates a comfortingly supportive 'we' which is able simply to dismiss any worries and thereby reduce anxiety and conflict, thereby making everyone feel good about themselves. Imagine, for instance, that Godfrey came back with his story from his visit to Daniel's family, and his supervisor accepted his account completely at face value, thanked him for a job well done, and agreed that the referral was obviously a malicious one which could safely be disregarded. Godfrey would be heartily relieved, and would also feel validated by his supervisor's acceptance of his story. His supervisor might also be relieved that she had one less case to allocate. Neither of them would have to deal with the discomfort that they might both feel if the supervisor had sharply questioned his account.

But this would not really be supervision at all. The supervisor would be adding nothing whatever to the value of Godfrey's assessment, and would in fact be reinforcing poor, and potentially dangerous, practice. This would merely be a pretence at supervision, much in the same way that Godfrey's visit was (in many ways) a pretence at an investigation.

One could argue, therefore, that the aim of good supervision should be to create an environment in which something like the opposite of groupthink takes place:

- There should not be ideas that can't be expressed
- Conclusions should not be reached prematurely
- Feelings and their implications should be considered, and no one should be made to feel bad simply for having feelings
- All the information available should be open to challenge, regardless of its source, and no information should be disregarded simply because of its source
- Disagreement should be welcomed as a way of interrogating the available information
- Even if the parties seem to agree, they should actively search for possible objections to their position, or gaps in their knowledge.

CONCLUDING NOTES FOR SUPERVISORS AND SUPERVISEES

Notes for supervisors (including practice educators)

The point of this chapter has been that your understanding about what is going on in the cases you are responsible for, is largely dependent on the quality of your interaction with your supervisees.

An overly cosy, reassuring supervision environment in which the supervisee's 'story' is unchallenged (a 'permissive' style of supervision, in the terms of Chapter 4), will yield poor quality information, because it leaves untouched the supervisee's various defences, evasions and blind spots, and will not support the development of the supervisee as a practitioner.

But an overly directive, 'authoritarian' environment will also yield poor quality information because it is unlikely to be conducive to the sharing of doubts and other uncomfortable feelings, or to real debate. What this chapter has been about is the creation of an 'authoritative' supervision environment, in which open discussion is possible.

Recognising the power both of feelings and of the various manoeuvres and defences we use to distance ourselves from uncomfortable feelings is important in supervision. This is not to say that supervision needs to 'wallow' in emotion – certainly not – but alertness to feelings is important, as is a willingness to name your own feelings, and to notice and comment on signs of powerful feelings in the other person: if someone looks tense, or seems to be trying to avoid talking about something, this is worth commenting on, and we should resist the normal social convention of pretending not to notice such things.

You may need to discuss the kinds of powerful feelings that are normal in this kind of work, in order to free your supervisee up to talk about them, since people do not necessarily recognise that these are appropriate things to bring up in a work context, and may feel ashamed of some of their emotional reactions until they realise they are common and normal.

The emphasis on feelings in this chapter should not be taken to suggest that feelings are more important than 'facts'. Facts are very important – you need to be as clear as you can be about what was done and what was not done, what was said and what was not said, so that you can get gaps filled and uncertainties clarified – but in human services like social work, you need to be aware of feelings in order to understand what the facts are telling you.

Notes for supervisees (including students on placement)

When I teach supervisors, I always mention the 'quiet door knock' of a social worker who rather dreads doing a visit. You knock very quietly, and then leave quickly, returning to the office to write down in the recording system that you visited but no one was in. They always know at once what I mean.

I'm not saying that the quiet door knock is good practice, or is something you should emulate. It's a pretty silly thing to do, and you'll only end up having to do the visit again another time anyway. My point is that your kind of work can be frightening at times for most of the people that do it, and we all, at some time or another, have engaged in silly manoeuvres and mind-games to avoid uncomfortable experiences.

You should feel free in supervision to talk about feelings, including negative ones, and about the way they may have affected your thinking. Recognising your feelings, and learning that they can both show you things and hide things from you, is a very important skill. If your supervisor is uncomfortable with this kind of material, you probably need to find someone else to talk to, but I hope your supervisor *will* talk to you about feelings and mind-games, and allow you to talk about them.

You should be aware that a good supervisor will challenge you, ask you for evidence to back up your statements, ask you why you didn't do or didn't ask certain things on

(Continued)

a visit. This can feel uncomfortable. It can feel as if you are being criticised or reprimanded, even if you aren't (just as your clients may feel when you question *them*). But actually you and your supervisor have a shared interest in getting it right – as, of course, do your clients – and sharp, interrogative questioning is a better way of achieving that, than simply listening to what you have to say. Supervision is work, and not a social encounter, and you should bear in mind that different rules apply.

CHAPTER SUMMARY

My starting point in this chapter was the fact that a supervisor generally knows a lot less about a case than the person she is supervising. She is trying to 'oversee' work that she hasn't seen. Most of the rest of the chapter has been about the ways in which the 'story' that is brought to the supervisor may be inaccurate or incomplete. What is actually there, what is noticed, what is remembered, what is deemed important, and what the supervisee decides she ought to talk about are all very different things.

I discussed 'gut feelings' which, on the one hand, are a very ancient, biological way of assessing a situation ('System 1'), but which, on the other, are often inaccurate because they are based on forming instant associations between things in the present and things in the past. Gut feelings are important to notice, but cannot simply be taken at face value.

I then looked at psychological defences against powerful negative feelings, and how they can have the effect of preventing us from seeing things that are actually there, or giving us a very distorted picture of what is there. One phenomenon that can occur in your kind of work is countertransference (I offered 'over-involvement' or 'over-identification' if you don't like the word), and I talked about the way in which this can result in individuals taking very rigid positions in which some characters are seen as victims, others as persecutors and others as rescuers.

I suggested that all this stuff going on in the background constitutes a kind of 'back story' to the story a supervisee tells to a supervisor about her work, and that one of the functions of supervision is trying to see this back story and think about how it may have modified or distorted the story that is being told.

I reviewed some of the powerful feelings that are in play in this kind of work, including fear, pity and horror, but also anger and punitiveness, and perhaps powerful feelings of warmth and even romantic love. I concluded by talking about the phenomenon of 'groupthink' and suggested that this represents the opposite of what supervision should be about.

The next chapter will look at the part of supervision where we start to draw conclusions and move towards a plan of action.

6

JUDGEMENTS OF SOLOMON

CONTENTS

> Making a decision involves making a choice between different possible courses of action and committing oneself to one of them; the choice being made in the absence of full factual information about the effects of the choice. If the facts were fully known, no decision need be made; the proper course of action would be self-evident. All decisions are thus necessarily attended by some uncertainty as to their outcome and consequently by some conflict and anxiety ... [which] is likely to be acute if a decision affects the treatment and welfare of patients. (Menzies, 1960: 104)

The above quote summarises rather well, I think, what is challenging about making decisions in situations where you can't be certain you've made the right choice, and where the wrong choice could have serious consequences, but a choice must still be made. It comes from Isabel Menzies' study of hospital nurses, but it is applicable to any professional working with human situations, including health visitors, youth workers, GPs, police officers, judges, social workers and even politicians. One might even argue that making such decisions is the *function* of professionals, and distinguishes professional activity from other more routinized tasks. As Menzies says, if the proper course of action was self-evident from the facts, no professional judgement would be needed.

The previous chapter looked at the first half of supervision cycle: how we tease out what has been said, done, heard, seen and felt. This chapter will look at the second half of the supervision cycle: how we come up with a coherent, useful and defensible picture of what is going on in a case ('Analysis' in the terminology of Wonnacott, 2012) and how we decide what to do about it ('Action planning').

What I want to show in this chapter is that analysis, and the action planning that flows from it, is about asking the right kinds of questions.

THE ANALYSIS DEFICIT

We don't always do the analysis part very well – or we don't in social work, at least. In Chapter 1, I cited the study Wilkins et al. (2017), based on transcripts of supervision sessions in a 'children in need' social work team, in which they identified a common pattern in which a 'verbal deluge' of detail provided by the supervisee (2017: 944) was followed by the supervisor identifying the 'problem' and providing a 'solution' with a 'tendency for the advice to concern procedural actions such as completing paperwork or arranging a meeting' (2017: 946): in other words, the social worker describes the Experience, but the Reflection and Analysis elements of supervision are skipped in order to arrive, not really even at an Action Plan, but at some procedural instructions.

Social workers are aware of this deficit. In a survey of 315 social workers by David Wilkins and Vivi Antonopoulou, '244 (77%) respondents said supervision helped with management over-sight, 185 (59%) said it helped with task clarity and 203 (64%) said it helped with adherence to timescales', but the number who said supervision helped with *analysis* was 86 – only 27% of those asked (2019: 28). As Wilkins and Antonopoulou observe:

> many respondents said supervision is 'most helpful' for management oversight and accountability and 'least helpful' for decision-making, emotional support, analysis and reflection. It would have been better to find the exact opposite and it is hard to see how supervision that focuses on management oversight and accountability to the exclusion of much else can ever be truly helpful for people who use services. (2019: 36)

Actually, I would question whether supervision can *really* deliver even management oversight and accountability if it does not also engage with 'decision-making, emotional support, analysis and reflection'. For, surely, in order to genuinely share accountability, the manager has to gain some understanding of the thinking that lies behind the practitioner's actions? How can you take line management responsibility for actions you don't understand?

Analysis may sometimes be skipped over in supervision because of lack of time, though this is a false economy, since poorly thought-through plans won't work, and will therefore waste a great deal of time in the long run. But, as I made clear in Chapter 2, my own view is that a large part of the problem lies in the fact that analysis and action planning are frightening, because once we come to a conclusion and act on it, we expose ourselves to the possibility of being wrong. Here, for instance, are some thoughts about the process from a focus group in which I was involved with social workers talking about their experience of care proceedings:

> '... even though you're not the only one that makes that decision, you feel that you're playing God'.
>
> '... you really are playing God, and it's the most horrible feeling'.
>
> 'These are judgements of Solomon at times, you know, and we do make them, and that is so scary'.
>
> '... I've only got little shoulders'. (Taylor et al., 2008: 26)

Given these anxieties, it can seem very tempting to avoid for as long as possible the process that will result in a conclusion and an action plan. Isabel Menzies suggested that one of the strategies that medical professionals used to deal with the anxiety aroused by uncertain choices was 'postponing action as long as possible' (1960: 104).

This is of course ultimately a self-defeating strategy, a bit like putting off going to the dentist about a painful tooth because you are afraid of the drill. Sooner or later the drill has to be faced.

WHAT ARE WE DEALING WITH HERE?

You are a supervisor. Your supervisee has been discussing a case with you. She has gathered a fair amount of information. She has read previous case notes. She has met the service users on many occasions and sought their own views, and she has made her own observations about their home circumstances, their interactions, their attitudes. She has discussed the case with other professionals and gathered their views. You have asked her about her 'gut feelings' about the case and, if necessary, explored these with her in the ways discussed in the previous chapter. Now you and she need to think about what needs to happen next, and for this to happen, you need first to come to a decision about what all this information so far seems to be *telling you*. After all, there is no point in collecting information *unless* it is used to draw conclusions of some kind and, while all of us might sometimes wish there was a 'grown-up' we could take all this stuff to and be told what to do, in reality we *are* the grown-ups.

So you and your supervisee, both in the supervision session and outside of it, need to ask yourselves questions like the following:

- *Needs.* Are there unmet needs in this situation which require addressing by our agency? What are they?
- *Risks.* Is anyone at risk, and what is the nature of the risks?
- *Capacity.* Is there anyone in this situation who lacks the capacity to make his or her own judgements? (The word 'capacity' is usually used in connection with adult service users who, for whatever reason, do not possess the ability to weigh up the options for themselves. However, the same question arises with children and young people who may lack the emotional maturity and life experience to come to such judgements.)
- *Mandate.* What is it about this situation that makes it appropriate for us to be involved?
- *Strengths/support/protective factors.* What positive factors are there in this situation? (Just as important to think about as negative ones.)
- *Relationships/significant others.* Who else is involved other than the primary service user or service users, what is the nature of their relationship? (Other people such as family members, neighbours and friends, are potential sources of support and strength, but may also be potential sources of danger. And they may also have needs of their own which will have to be addressed if they are to play a part.)

These are all 'what are we dealing with here?' kinds of questions.

The difficult thing about such questions is that answers cannot simply be 'read off' from the information that has been gathered in the way that you can read off the dials on the control panel of your car. No matter how much detail has been gathered about the people concerned, the information on its own will not simply tell you (for instance) how much risk of harm there is to the service user. (It may be obvious in a few extreme cases, but in most cases it is impossible to be sure.) Nor is there a formula into which you can simply feed the 'data' and get an answer. You and your supervisee need to decide for yourselves what the information is telling you. You need to come to a professional judgement. (Or, if the supervisee feels she has already come to a judgement, you as supervisor need to check it.)

This can be challenging. Part of the problem is that the information you have is necessarily incomplete. As we discussed at the beginning of the previous chapter, the information available to the practitioner is never the whole story about a service user's life, but rather a snapshot, seen from a particular viewpoint. Awareness that you do not have the whole picture can lead to a decision to postpone decisions until more information is gathered and of course this is often appropriate, but more information is not always what's needed. This is because,

a *'Saturation'*. You can *never* get the whole picture, and a point comes when new information doesn't really add to what you already know. Qualitative researchers refer to this as the 'saturation point' (see, for instance, Saunders et al., 2018).

b *Timeliness*. Postponing a decision *is of itself a decision*, and it may have harmful consequences. Writing about legal proceedings to do with the care of children, Goldstein et al. (1980) pointed out that to wait for absolute certainty as to what is going on for a child would mean never coming to a decision at all. The possibility of making the wrong decision would thus be avoided, but the child's whole childhood would have passed in a state of not knowing where she belonged.

So the challenge faced by supervisee and supervisor is that they must come to the best possible judgement about 'what we are dealing with here' while recognising that this judgement must be made within a certain timescale (the appropriate timescale will depend on the situation and may be measured in minutes in some cases, and in years in others), and on the basis of information which is necessarily not completely comprehensive. (It must also usually be made in the absence of a completely objective method of evaluating and interpreting information.) This can be very difficult for the supervisee, the supervisor, or both, and can result, as Bill McKitterick notes, in 'analysis paralysis' (2012: 65): an inability to come to any decision at all for fear of making the wrong call. Table 6.1 summarises some of the symptoms of this common condition.

Table 6.1 Symptoms of analysis paralysis

Supervisee suffering from analysis paralysis	Supervisee is 'stuck in Experience' or 'stuck in Reflection' (see Chapter 2), willing to rehearse either what they have seen/heard, or what they felt, but unwilling to draw any conclusions. * In order to avoid reaching conclusions, supervisee may ensure that negative and positives of service user's situation are carefully balanced, even if this requires 'overegging' or underplaying one or the other. * Supervisee presents 'undigested' material and invites supervisor to say what it means. * Having invited the supervisor to say what the material means, supervisee may then be reluctant to accept what supervisor says, and raise objections to any suggested interpretation. * Sometimes social workers and social work students may be paralysed in part by a misapprehension about social work ethics. They may fear coming to a judgement for fear of being 'judgemental' or 'discriminatory'.
Supervisor suffering from analysis paralysis	In the guise of supporting supervisee's own thinking, supervisor questions supervisee about experience and perhaps feelings, but does not ask 'what are we dealing with?' questions, and does not offer suggestions, so that the supervisee emerges from supervision without having developed her thinking. * Supervisor retreats behind bureaucracy, for example by suggesting meetings that should happen, asking supervisee to consult with others, or insisting on referring the decision-making process to other forums. (It may be appropriate to call a meeting, or course, but the supervisor should still be helping the supervisee to decide what she wants from that meeting, and what she will say at it.) * Supervisor avoids dealing with main issue by focusing on procedural aspects. (For instance, instead of discussing the content of an assessment, focusing entirely on the time it was completed in, or the format that was used to record it.)
Supervisee and supervisor suffering from analysis paralysis	Both parties may collude in focusing on peripheral or irrelevant aspects of the case under discussion, and may agree together to pass on the decision-making to others, or to additional forums. * Or they may agree to carry out additional assessment exercises long after the point where an outside observer would say that 'saturation point' has been reached. * If both are theoretically inclined, they may indulge in lengthy and perhaps enjoyable discussions about the theoretical and ethical implications of the case, while avoiding coming to any usable conclusions.

None of the above is meant to suggest that it isn't often appropriate to consult more widely, or keep an open mind for a longer period, or carry out additional assessments. Nevertheless, a key function of supervision should be to ensure that the 'what are we dealing with here?' questions are addressed, and not postponed indefinitely. After all, even if it is appropriate to consult others, we need to go to those others with some thoughts of our own. Even if it is appropriate to carry out further assessments, these will be more productive if we have generated some hypotheses which further assessments could confirm, discount or modify.

Why do you say that?

'Why do you say that?' – or variants of it such as 'What makes you think that?' 'What evidence are you basing that on?' 'Why do you think explanation X fits better than explanation Y?' – is another kind of 'What are we dealing with?' question. Thus, if the answer to 'Is anyone at risk here?' is 'Yes, I think Mrs Brown is at risk of financial abuse by her daughter-in-law, Mrs Thomas?', the next question should be something like 'Why do you say that?' or 'What evidence do we have that this is the case?' These questions put the supervisee in the position of having to defend her judgement: does she really have any evidence that Mrs Thomas is financially abusing her mother-in-law, or is she just talking about a 'gut feeling'? (If it is the latter, then, as we discussed in the previous chapter, it still needs to be explored: it *may* be an indicator that the practitioner has picked up a 'vibe' of something bad that's going on and needs looking into further, but it may not, and you need more than a hunch if you are going to act.) Having elicited the evidence which the supervisee feels supports her conclusion, it is then possible to discuss how strong it is, and whether other interpretations are possible or more likely. Analysis paralysis is less likely to occur if the evidence is properly put to the test.

Why is this happening?

'Why is this happening?' – expressed in various ways – is another kind of 'What are we dealing with?' question. This encourages a more dynamic way of thinking, because you are moving on from discussing what the service user's risks and needs are *right now*, to thinking about *why* things are the way they are. Suppose your supervisee thinks baby Tom is at risk of neglect from his lone parent mother. Suppose you have already asked what form the risk will take – let us say your supervisee has evidence that the mother leaves the baby to cry for long periods, feeds him sweets to keep him quiet, and changes Tom's nappy so infrequently that he has a more or less chronic nappy rash – you now need to explore *why* his mother does this.

As you explore this question, you are starting to come up with a kind of theory. And you often need to have some sort of theory about why something is happening in order to know what to do about it, much in the same way that a doctor needs to know, not just the fact that a patient has a painful rash, but what may be *causing* that rash, before she can know what course of treatment is likely to be effective. Perhaps Tom's mother is clinically depressed ... Perhaps she has a learning disability and finds it hard to understand what a baby needs ... Perhaps Tom reminds her of his abusive father and she can hardly bear to touch him ... Whatever the reason, Tom is still being neglected, but each of these explanations would suggest an entirely different course of action.

In other words, 'Why is this happening?' questions – which are part of the broader category of 'What are we dealing with?' questions – help us to know what we need to think about as we move from analysis to action planning. They may also indicate important gaps in our knowledge that require further enquiry.

EXERCISE 6.1

Encouraging analysis

In the previous paragraphs I've given the example of Tom who is being neglected by his mother. How would you as a supervisor encourage a supervisee to explore the reasons for this in supervision? Or, looking at this from the perspective of a supervisee, what would you need from your supervisor to encourage you to think about the reasons?

Clearly you need to move on at some point from purely factual questions like 'How bad was the nappy rash?' or 'How often has he been heard crying like that?' It's likely that the mother will have given her own explanations for how things are, in which case you'd need to explore how well it fits with the rest of what you know. It may well be that, when asked about gut feelings, the supervisee has already come up with a possible answer to the 'Why is this happening?' question (for instance: 'I just don't think she really wants to be responsible for him at all'), in which case you would need to go back to ask 'Why do you say that?', 'What makes you think that?' etc.

But sometimes supervisees can be reluctant to commit themselves to any particular conclusion, in which case you could ask them to list all the possibilities and evaluate them. The important part is to express curiosity as to the possibilities, and to avoid shutting down discussion too quickly by (for instance) jumping straight onto procedural matters like when a case conference should be called, or whether the case record is fully up to date on the agency's information system. After all, calling a case conference does not avoid the 'Why is this happening?' question, it just defers it.

THEORIES, KNOWLEDGE, 'THEORY'

Since we are now talking about forming theories about what is going on in a case, it is important, at least briefly, to consider the role of formal 'theory', by which I mean formal bodies of ideas that you can draw upon in coming to an answer to 'What are we dealing with here?' questions (and also, as we'll discuss later) to 'What are we going to do?' questions.

Sometimes these bodies of ideas might best be described not as 'theories' but as knowledge. For instance, if you are working with someone suffering with Alzheimer's Disease you need to possess, or have access to, a reasonable amount of knowledge of the effects of this condition, and its long-term prognosis, if you are to understand what is going on and come up with reasonable plans. Likewise if you are working with someone with drinking problems, or someone who is a victim of domestic violence, or someone who has perpetrated sexual abuse, there are bodies of knowledge to which the professional needs to have access (though we should not underestimate the extent to which such knowledge can be debatable and contested). You cannot just rely on 'common sense' when dealing with such situations.

Social work students are not taught all that much detailed 'knowledge' in the above sense. I suspect students in other disciplines are taught rather more. However, social work students *are* taught 'social work theory' (most of it actually comes from other disciplines), and there are many books about the subject including one by me (Howe, 2009; Payne, 2014; Beckett and Horner, 2015; Maclean and Harrison, 2015; etc.). 'Theory' in a field like social work is a *sort* of knowledge, but it's not knowledge in the same way that information about the known long-term effects of Alzheimer's is knowledge. It's much less specific and much more contested. Social work practice educators often worry about 'theory' and sometimes express anxiety that their student supervisees may think they are not sufficiently up on 'theory' in this sense. Students and newly qualified workers may feel that the 'theory' they've been taught, however convincing it seemed at the time, doesn't really provide clear answers to the real world questions their assessments are supposed to address.

But the 'theories' discussed in social work training – and in the training for other similar professions such as youth work, teaching or nursing, I would imagine – *do* have value because they encourage the skill of looking at human situations in different ways and recognising influences on human behaviour and thinking that are not necessarily obvious. 'Theories' do not generate straightforward answers, but by naming 'theories' and therefore recognising that there are a range of different ones, we make it easier to see the 'frame' we are using when we are talking about a case, rather than just assuming that our own way of thinking is the only way to look at things. What's key is not that you can name, and reproduce by rote, terminology that you learnt on your professional training, but rather that you are able to look at human behaviour from a number of different angles when trying to answer 'What are we dealing with here?' questions.

What's important is not that either supervisee or supervisor should be able to reproduce 'parrot fashion' all the detail of 'theories' learnt in the past, but that supervision session should be a place where competent *theorising* can take place – and a place where the skill of theorising is nurtured and developed. Asking 'What are we dealing with?', 'Why do you say that?' and 'Why is this happening?' bring you naturally into this territory.

What I find helpful to remember is that the various 'theories' or 'models' that you can find in the literature usually correspond with ideas that have either always been, or have become, general currency: ideas that form part of the 'toolkit' of most people to varying degrees. In Table 6.2, I illustrate six broad 'perspectives' (for want of a better word) into which I think most of what are called social work 'theories' can be grouped. And all of these 'perspectives' can also be found in everyday language and everyday experience. For instance, if we were discussing a child whose behaviour was difficult we might say the parents were not setting proper boundaries ('present perspective'), we might mention some traumatic experience he had had ('past perspective'), or we might possibly even suggest that he was behaving in a demanding way to bring his parents together and stop them fighting with one another ('systems perspective'). If a friend was trying to make up her mind to make a big change in her life, we might encourage her to believe in herself ('future perspective'). And so on.

Table 6.2 Contrasting 'perspectives' on human problems

'Perspective'	Key insight	Examples
Past-oriented perspective	Past experience has major influence on present functioning (and present experience has a major impact on future development)	• Attachment theory (especially the idea of the internalised 'working model') • Other psychodynamic theories • Any therapeutic approach that focuses on psychological recovery from past hurt
Present-oriented perspective	Individual behaviour is shaped and maintained by positive or negative reinforcers in their present environment	• Behavioural training for children • Cognitive Behavioural Therapy (with focus on identifying 'triggers' etc.)
Future-oriented perspective	People change when they believe a different future is possible	• Solution-focused therapy and its offshoots (emphasis on visualising the future, and noticing instances where it is already present) • Strengths perspective • Task-centred approach (aimed at making change more manageable) • Person-centred therapy (emphasis on creating change-conducive therapeutic environment)

'Perspective'	Key insight	Examples
Systems perspective	Human behaviour is best understood in terms of the functioning of the family (or other group) of which they are a member	• Various different models of 'family therapy' and 'family systems' approaches
Political/ social perspective	Human behaviour needs to be understood in the context of society, including people's material circumstances, cultural context, and oppression or discrimination they may be facing	• Rights-based perspectives • Feminist perspectives • Disability rights perspective • Focus on advocacy rather than personal change
Practical perspective	Sometimes people just need practical help with life's problems	• Focus on provision of practical services, such as aids and adaptations, financial assistance, day care, home care, alternative care provision

There is no reason why all of the different 'perspectives' in Table 6.2 might not be equally valid ways of looking at the same situation (in many cases they are). They do not contradict one another (in the same way that 'The car is going very fast because the driver is late for an appointment' and 'The car is going very fast because the accelerator is right down on the floor' do not contradict one another, they just describe different aspects of the situation). But people tend to have their favourites, depending partly on their own life experience. For instance people from unhappy but materially comfortable middle-class backgrounds may pick up on the psychological factors in a situation, and on the legacy of past events that service users are dealing with but, since they have no experience of it, they can be less perceptive to the impact of poverty, or of (say) living in a poor neighbourhood with high crime rates and few opportunities. Someone who has grown up in such an environment, on the other hand, may focus very much on those environmental factors, which are very real to her, and perhaps focus less on the purely psychological ones. In the same way, women are usually more sensitive than men to misogyny and sexism in a situation, Black people better able than white people to understand the effects of racism on people's lives.

So, while one of the functions of supervision must be to explore cases within the framework of a given perspective ('What are we dealing with?', for instance, may include trying to get a sense of the effect on a parent of her own abusive childhood), another function must be to open up the possibility that it might be helpful to look at the case from another whole 'perspective', including perspectives which the supervisee – or supervisor – feels less at home with. You can do this by deliberately asking 'Why is this happening?' questions that focus on particular 'perspectives': 'What aspects of this person's history may be contributing to her behaviour?' 'What is there about living in this particular housing estate that may be contributing to this problem?'

A SAFE SPACE

'Theory' in the formal sense of 'social work theory' (or 'youth work theory' etc.) is valuable, but a crucial task of supervision is to come up with 'theories' in the more everyday sense of 'My theory about this is that ...' The word 'hypothesis' could also be used. We sometimes speak of a 'working hypothesis' to mean our theory about what is going on that we are currently using as the basis for action, while recognising that it may need to be modified or replaced at some point in the light of new developments.

For instance, in a case of a non-accidental injury to, say, an elderly person with dementia, you need to have some sort of hypothesis about what might have happened and why, in order to take appropriate action. Was this a one-off loss of control by a very stressed but otherwise loving carer? Or was it a calculated attempt to hurt and intimidate by a so-called carer who doesn't really care at all? Those two possibilities could result in the exact same injury, but they are very different situations and would indicate very different kinds of intervention.

When the supervisor is much more experienced than the supervisee, she may feel that she has grasped what's going on long before the supervisee. The temptation then is simply to tell the supervisee that 'What you are dealing with is X', or even to skip that stage and simply tell the supervisee what to do next (see Chapter 2 on 'short-circuiting' the supervisory cycle). But of course this would deprive the supervisee of an opportunity to come up with hypotheses of her own in a safe environment and to receive feedback on them, thus denying her an opportunity to develop her analytical skills. The service as a whole will lose out if those who have most contact with its users are denied the opportunity to develop professional judgement. So, except in emergencies, it's important that supervisors hold back and ask questions, rather than just imposing their own thinking.

It is worth noting that, while 'analysis paralysis' can often be the result of being afraid of coming to the wrong decision, it can also be the result of social embarrassment. Inexperienced supervisees – students and newly qualified staff – may be particularly reluctant to offer thoughts about 'What are we dealing with?' out of a fear that their ideas may seem naïve and ill-informed or even ridiculous to a more experienced and knowledgeable supervisor. It can also happen that supervisees are reluctant to offer views such as 'X is not parenting her children adequately' for fear of seeming judgemental or discriminatory. So it is important that supervisors create an environment in supervision in which it is OK to be wrong, and fine to throw out ideas for discussion, even if they are likely to be quickly discarded. For, if thoughts are not spoken out loud, they can't be explored, developed or ruled out.

One of the great benefits of supervision is that it allows for a 'dry run'. Ideas can be tested in the safe space of a supervision session, without risk to the service user. So supervision can serve a function a little like that of a flight simulator for a pilot:

you can try things out without the risk of crashing the plane in the process. But unless supervision feels safe enough for the supervisee (a) to be honest, and (b) to express thoughts which she knows might show up her naïvety or inexperience, it cannot serve that function.

BRINGING IT ALL TOGETHER

Figure 6.1 is an attempt to represent something of the process that needs to go on, both in supervision and in the heads of those involved, between the gathering of information about a case, and the formation of an action plan. In this diagram, the four dark circles relate to the four elements of the Wonnacott supervisory cycle presented in Chapter 2: Experience, Reflection, Analysis and Action Planning. 'Facts' constitute the material explored as 'Experience' (though, as we discussed in Chapter 2, 'Facts' are not the straightforward matter they appear to be at first sight). 'Intuitions' are the feelings that are the subject of 'Reflection'. 'Theories/Hypotheses' are the goal of 'Analysis'. And they in turn will be the basis of 'Action Planning'. My diagram stops there, but in fact Action Planning results in actions of one kind or another, which leads to new facts requiring consideration, and then the whole cycle begins again.

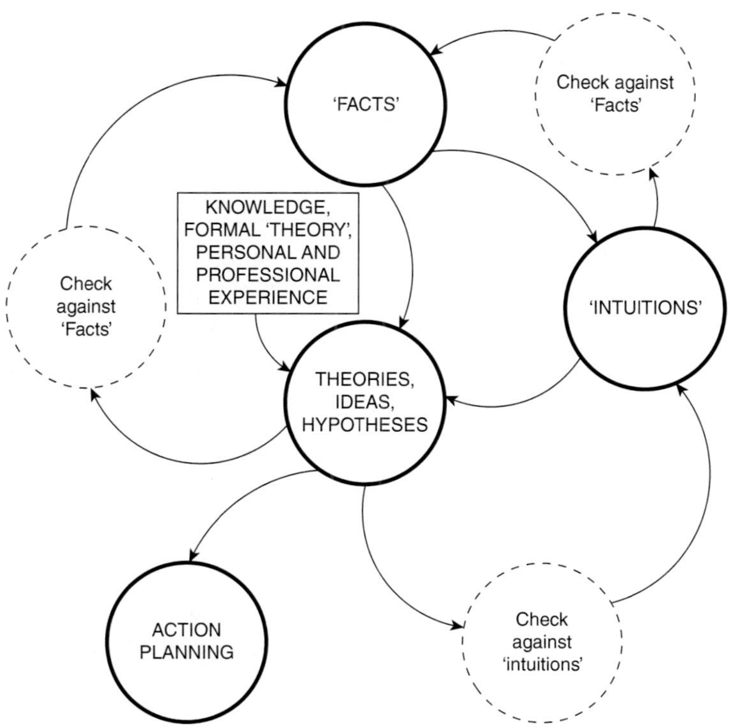

Figure 6.1 The process of analysis

But, please note, though I have said that 'Theories/Hypotheses' are the *goal* of Analysis, the diagram *as a whole* represents the *process* of Analysis. Much more is going on as we come to judgements than a straightforward one-directional cycle:

- Intuitions need to be checked back against facts. Are our intuitions supported by the facts? Are they telling us that there are more facts which we haven't attended to? Or do the facts show us that our feelings are groundless?
- Theories and hypotheses need to be checked back against the facts. Is our idea about what is happening here consistent with what we know? Are there more things we need to find out?
- Theories and hypotheses should be checked against intuitions too. Do our conclusions *feel* right? If not, why not? And if they *do* feel right, are we sure that we haven't just constructed a theory to confirm our possibly mistaken gut feelings?
- Theories and hypotheses need to be informed by appropriate knowledge, and perhaps should make use of formal 'theory', as well as drawing on experience.

WHAT ARE WE GOING TO DO?

So now we come to the Action Planning stage. Sometimes we conclude there's nothing further to do be done. Otherwise, action can take a number of forms, which will be a combination of the following:

1 *Further assessment.* Sometimes it's important to recognise that you just don't have enough information.
2 *Further discussion.* Sometimes it's appropriate (or required by procedural rules) to defer decision-making about what is going on and what should be done about it to another forum, such as a planning meeting or case conference.
3 *Intervention.* This is of course what your agency exists to provide: an action that has a direct impact on the service user in order to make a difference, hopefully for the better. In many cases it will involve providing practical services. In others it will involve the supervisee doing some work with the service user herself. In some cases it will involve invoking legal powers to impose some kind of change.

It's important to remember that, if further assessment, further discussion, or both, are chosen as the action plan, without any actual intervention, then there will be no immediate change in the life of the service user. An assessment isn't an alternative to providing a service, nor is a planning meeting, and calling a case conference does not in itself reduce risk, even though it may reduce professional anxiety. These options are only justified if there is a reasonable expectation that they will result in a better intervention than would otherwise occur.

On the other hand, if an actual intervention is agreed upon, then further assessment and further discussion must *also* happen. If you intervene, you need to reflect on the consequences of the intervention, as these may or may not necessitate revising your plan. (Your doctor prescribes ointment for the rash on your arm, having formed the working hypothesis that you are suffering from condition X. But if the ointment makes no difference, she needs to revisit her hypothesis.)

If the decision made is to have further discussion in another forum such as a planning meeting, it's important to remember that participants in such a meeting need to come to it with ideas, about 'what is going on?' and about possible action plans, and not just show up.

Intervention

Assuming that a working hypothesis exists, we now come to intervention. Thoughts about what intervention is appropriate can actually be quite powerfully influenced by the feelings and 'perspectives' of supervisee and supervisor. I recently heard a supervisor talking about a relatively inexperienced social worker who was very keen to remove both children from a family and split them between two placements. This is a *very* drastic intervention, obviously, and the supervisor felt it was premature. I wondered if the supervisee's anxieties about the case meant that she was a little too ready to opt for a solution that would completely and finally dismantle the current circumstances which were making her very anxious (and which, perhaps, were exposing her own doubts about her practice skills)? Indeed, sometimes professionals are so anxious that 'something must be done' that they want to jump straight to very drastic action, with very little reflection or analysis at all (this is being 'stuck in Action' (see Chapter 2, p 34).

Other supervisees in the same situation, on the other hand, might be made so anxious about the idea of breaking up a family unit, that they might defer making a decision at all for as long as possible, even if the home situation was clearly harmful, and existing services were not making much difference.

Who are we really doing this for?

So when it comes to exploring possible interventions in supervision, it's important to ensure, not only that the plan is consistent with the working hypothesis (i.e. 'Are parenting classes likely to be helpful to Tom's mother, given what we think is going on for her?') but also that due reflection takes place about the intervention itself to ensure that it's meeting the needs of the service user and not just the needs of the supervisee or the supervisor or the professional system to manage their anxieties.

Therefore, one final check that needs to be applied to any plan for intervention (or indeed to any plan to *delay* an intervention) is 'Who are we really doing this for?' There are a number of possible beneficiaries whose needs an intervention can meet (remember the 'stakeholders' of supervision discussed in Chapter 2), but not all of these needs are legitimate reasons for action. Table 6.3 is an attempt to sum this up.

Table 6.3 Beneficiaries of an intervention

Possible beneficiary	Possible benefit	Legitimate basis for intervention?
Primary service user	Meets a need, reduces a risk, protects against harm, improves quality of life	Yes. This is supposed to be the primary purpose for which human service agencies exist.
Secondary service users (carers of primary service user, parents of primary service user etc.)	Meets a need, reduces a risk, protects against harm, improves quality of life	Yes, if their needs are deemed to be sufficient to make them primary service users in their own right.
	Helps them provide better care for primary service user	Yes. This is very often by far the best way of meeting the needs of the primary service user (for instance: helping an elderly man cope better with the care of his wife, by giving him space to get some rest).
Wider community	Protecting wider community from harm	Yes. For instance, detaining someone in a mental hospital because they are thought to be a danger to the public. In some cases protecting the community may be the main purpose of the agency (for instance: youth justice services aim to prevent crime).
	Protecting wider community from minor inconvenience or feelings of discomfort	No. For instance, it is not OK to remove an elderly person to an institution, if she has capacity and knows the risks she's taking, just because neighbours find her worrying and would rather she was somewhere else.
Other primary service users	Protecting other service users from harm	Yes. For instance, moving a young person from a children's home where he is assaulting other residents.
	Freeing up resources for other service users	Yes, but … For instance, it may be justified to move an elderly person out of a hospital bed where she would like to stay until she felt better, if there are other people who need the bed more. But clearly this depends on how harmful it would be to move her.

Possible beneficiary	Possible benefit	Legitimate basis for intervention?
Professionals (including supervisee and supervisor)	Reducing anxieties, making professional feel better	No. It's not appropriate to intervene in someone's life to make professionals feel better, unless that intervention is legitimate for other reasons. Sometimes formal and procedural steps can be taken that will reduce professional anxieties without impacting on the service user. Sometimes an intervention may have to be chosen to fit in with what a professional is able to deliver, but that is a matter of managing resources not of meeting the professional's personal needs.
The organisation/agency	Protecting reputation of organisation	No. It's not appropriate to intervene in someone's life just so an organisation can cover its back. But the organisation's reputation is important, and does impact on its ability to deliver a service, and sometimes formal/procedural steps need to be taken in order to protect it.

CONCLUDING NOTES FOR SUPERVISORS AND SUPERVISEES

Notes for supervisors (including practice educators)

The key point here is that supervision adds no value to a case in terms of professional practice unless it includes 'What is going on here?' type questions. To simply hear the situation and then talk purely in terms of procedural steps serves a managerial purpose perhaps, but it misses out the essential clinical component of supervision. (It would be as if two doctors were to discuss a set of symptoms without even thinking about possible diagnoses.) A human service agency exists to provide a service in the form of various kinds of intervention, and it is only possible to choose an intervention by trying to understand the situation under discussion. This point may seem too obvious to make, but research suggests that supervision in reality is often not very good at this, as discussed at the beginning of this chapter.

Key to getting it right is asking the right questions. There is a set of questions which we use to draw out the facts, and another set of questions we can ask to draw out the gut feelings and the emotional responses which are so important to understand, but there is also a distinct set of questions – questions on the lines of 'What are we dealing with here?' 'Why do you say that?' 'Why is this happening?' – which lead towards the formation of some kind of theory or working hypothesis about a case.

(Continued)

Without such a working hypothesis it is not possible to come up with a useful action plan (except perhaps in a few very basic situations where what is going on is simply obvious!). With a hypothesis it becomes possible to think about what needs to be addressed, and how.

In order to develop the best possible working hypothesis, and in order to help your supervisees develop their own analytical skills, you need to create a safe space in supervision where ideas can be discussed without fear, and where speculation is not only permitted but encouraged.

Notes for supervisees (including students on placement)

When I became a social worker, and for many years afterwards, I used to feel guilty about the fact that I would visit people and gather information about them, but rarely had a clear sense of what I needed to do. If I was a better social worker, I felt, the answer would come to me like a flash of light. As I progressed in my career, though, I came to realise that it doesn't work like that. There are seldom real 'lightbulb moments' and, when they do come, they need to be treated with caution because they aren't necessarily correct. All you can normally hope for is some sort of working hypothesis or theory.

In order to arrive at such a theory, you need supervision that includes analysis. You need to be able to explore what you've seen, heard and felt, and find a way of making sense of it. You need to be able to discuss ideas, including ideas that turn out to be completely wrong. If there is no room for this in your supervision, you need to ask for it, or talk with your supervisor about finding other ways of getting it (see discussion in Chapter 3).

You cannot grow as a professional unless you are able to explore the information you gather in your assessments, and think about what it means. Indeed you haven't really *done* an assessment until you have done that thinking. In ordinary English, after all, when we talk about an 'assessment of a situation' we don't just mean a list of facts, we mean a judgement about what's going on. We mean an answer – even if only a provisional one – to the question, 'What are we dealing with here?'

Of course you can and should ask these questions of yourself outside of supervision ('What am I dealing with here?' 'Why do I think this?' 'Why is this particular set of problems occurring in this service user's life?'). But this is difficult to do with confidence in the early stages of your career – even when you are more experienced, you will still need to get the perspectives of others in order to check your thinking – so you need your supervisor to help you ask the right questions, and come up with reasonable answers.

In order to act you need a reasonable working hypothesis on which to act. You can seldom guarantee that a working hypothesis is correct, and you may need to revise it, but you do need a hypothesis that has been prodded and poked, considered from different angles, tested against the facts and your feelings … Supervision ought to give you an opportunity to do this.

When choosing an intervention, you do need to think carefully about whose benefit it really serves.

CHAPTER SUMMARY

This chapter started by acknowledging that the analytical element of supervision is, in practice, often weak. This is a serious problem because, without analysis, appropriate action cannot be chosen.

I have tried to demystify 'analysis' here by summing it up with the question 'What are we dealing with here?' It is this question, and questions like it, that allow us to form theories or hypotheses on which to act. Related questions are 'Why do you say that?' (which explores the evidence and thinking leading up to a theory or hypothesis) and 'Why is this happening?' (which explores the possible reasons for the behaviour of a service user, or of others, in the scenario being discussed).

Clearly knowledge is important here. (By way of illustration I used the example of a case where someone has Alzheimer's disease: you can't hope to come to a reasonable understanding of what's going on in such a case, unless you know – or have access to someone who knows – about the effects of Alzheimer's and its likely progression.) 'Theory', in the sense that the word is used on social work courses, has a part to play, though it is less specific. Its biggest benefit is that it makes you aware of different perspectives from which to look at things. However, the key thing at this stage is not 'theory' but the formation of a theory in the everyday sense – I also call it a working hypothesis – about what is going on in the situation being discussed.

I discussed the importance of a safe space in supervision, where ideas and speculations – even not very good ones – can be discussed and weighed up. This is important not only in order to come up with the best possible understanding, but also to support the development of the supervisee's analytical skills, and I talked about the process of bringing things together to arrive at a working hypothesis that can be used as a basis for action.

Finally, I discussed Action Planning. I made the distinction between purely procedural actions which do not, in themselves, impact on the service user's world, and substantive actions – interventions, services – which do impact on the service user's world and which are the purpose for which a human service agency exists. Interventions won't help unless they address the specific situation of the service user in question. This is why a working hypothesis is necessary.

I cautioned that interventions can meet needs of professionals as well as service users, and it is important to be clear about whose need is really being met by any intervention plan.

The next chapter moves away from the formal process of supervision to look at some of the interpersonal processes that may be happening at the same time.

7

GAMES WE ALL PLAY

CONTENTS

Whether or not you are currently in a supervisor role, I'd like you to begin this chapter by thinking about yourself as a supervis*ee*.

EXERCISE 7.1

Avoiding being told to do something

Imagine that you are going to supervision with a case or an issue that you know your supervisor will want to discuss. Imagine that there are two possible courses of actions for dealing with this case. Your preferred course of action is A, but you are aware of a different course of action, B, which you very much want to avoid having to do but can well imagine your supervisor preferring. (Exercise 5.1, on p 84, is a rather extreme example of a social worker in exactly that position, but try and think of a real situation you have experienced yourself.) How would you deal with this in supervision? How might you handle your presentation of the case or issue in a way to maximise the chances of getting the outcome you would prefer?

Obviously I can't speak for you, but I'm guessing you might do at least some of the following:

- Act like a defence lawyer. Present the arguments for A and the arguments for B in different ways which downplay the disadvantages of A and play up its advantages, while highlighting the disadvantages of B and minimising the advantages.
- Selectively present the evidence. I'm not saying that you would actually conceal things, or misrepresent the facts – though some supervisees probably would do so if they felt strongly enough – but, if it were me, I think I might provide more detail on the facts that support A. It's possible to do this without being conscious of it and without saying anything that could later be described as dishonest.
- Deliberately leave this case to the end of the agenda, when there is less time, and perhaps also ensure that you have been careful to defer to you supervisor's view on several other cases, so as to avoid any sense that you are resistant to, or disrespectful of, your supervisor's legitimate input.
- Act as if A has more or less been agreed already and only requires formal ratification, then move on to other cases on which (as above) you solicitously seek detailed guidance from your supervisor.
- Present the case in a way that flatters the supervisor, or makes A seem to fit in with their worldview. For instance: 'I'm pretty sure you're going to say X should remain at home because you are always so strong on defending people's

right to live in the community.' Or you could identify B with someone whose views you and your supervisor don't usually share: 'Dr X is arguing for B, but then he *always* does, doesn't he?!'

- Find ways of making your supervisor feel that your judgement on this matter is superior to hers: 'As you know, I've always had a special interest in this field', you might say, knowing quite well that your supervisor is not an expert on this particular matter, 'and I feel pretty confident that A is the right course of action'.
- Find ways of making your supervisor feel that A was pretty much her idea anyway: 'In our last supervision you were pretty keen on A, and I've been thinking a lot about it, and I'm sure you were absolutely right.'

You may feel that some of these are a little over the top, but I'm sure you'll agree, nevertheless, that we all approach such encounters equipped with various strategies for getting what we want – some of them more manipulative than others. Human service professionals typically have quite a lot of skill in this area because trying to persuade people to do things is very much part of their job.

Up to a point, such 'games' are inevitable and even necessary. Supervisees should have ideas and be keen to make the case for them. But supervisors do need to be aware that this is what is going on. It would be naïve for a supervisor to take what her supervisee says as simply the unbiased facts, and she should recognise that most of the time (and often without deliberate intent) what supervisees are doing is making out the case for their preferred interpretation of what is going on, their preferred course of action, their preferred agenda. And supervisors do need to be aware that some 'games' (such as flattery) are much more insidious than others: not just partisan argument, but the emotional equivalent of bribery or threats.

The same is true the other way round, of course. Supervisors too have personal agendas of various kinds, which may result in 'games' that get in the way of reaching the optimum decision. This chapter will look at the 'games' played by both sides, and the 'games' they play together.

THE IDEA OF 'GAMES'

Referring to these characteristic patterns of behaviour as 'games' originates with a famous text on Transactional Analysis by Eric Berne which first came out in 1964: *Games People Play* (2016). Probably the most well-known application of this idea in the field of supervision is by Alfred Kadushin in a paper (1999) first published in 1967, and then in a book on supervision which has since picked up a co-author and been through five editions (Kadushin, 1976; Kadushin and Harkness, 2014).

In my experience, some students on supervision courses are uncomfortable with the word 'game' which they feel carries too many connotations of cynical manipulation, so I'd like to make clear that 'games' in this sense are something that we all engage in to some extent as we try to get what we want or need, or avoid things we fear or dislike, and the person playing them may not even be conscious that playing games is what she's doing. Even when we are partly aware of the game we are playing (I'll drop the quote marks now) we are not usually deploying it in cold blood in a deliberate and calculated way, but rather falling into a pattern of behaviour which we repeat in an almost Pavlovian fashion because we've learnt in the past that it brings results.

GAMES SUPERVISEES PLAY

Coming first to the games that supervisees play, I defer to Kadushin's framework. He identifies a number of games to which he has given memorable and often amusing names, and he has grouped them into four categories as follows.

Manipulating demand

These games are aimed at deflecting unwelcome demands. For example the game Kadushin calls '*Two against the agency*' (1999: 57) is played by skilled practitioners who are good at face-to-face work and resent having to do paperwork – or these days, more likely, screenwork. How the game works is that the supervisee invites the supervisor to agree with her that all this bureaucracy takes time away from actual practice and encourages a tick-box approach which goes against all the values of the profession. Supervisors who have some sympathy with these views are then put in the position of either siding with the supervisee against the system, or going against their own beliefs in order to insist that the supervisee spend time on the bureaucracy that otherwise could have been spent with service users.

Another game is '*Be nice to me because I am nice to you*' (Kadushin, 1999: 57). This is basically just flattery. A supervisee playing this game says things like, '"You're the best supervisor I've ever had"' (1999: 57) and, as Kadushin notes:

> It is a game of emotional blackmail in which, having been paid in this kind of coin, the supervisor finds himself incapable of firmly holding the worker to legitimate demands. The supervisor finds it difficult to resist engaging in the game because it is gratifying to be regarded as an omniscient source of wisdom; there is satisfaction in being perceived as helpful and in being selected as a pattern for identification and emulation. (1999: 57)

He goes on to say that 'An invitation to play a game that tends to enhance a positive self-concept and feed one's narcissistic needs is likely to be accepted' (1999: 57). I'm not sure this is always true – some people really aren't very susceptible to this kind of thing at all – but it is a hard game to resist if you secretly have doubts as to your usefulness as a supervisor. And, just as Kadushin says, once you have been drawn in, it becomes much harder to challenge or criticise the supervisee.

Redefining the relationship

This group of games work by turning the supervisor–supervisee relationship into something else. In the game *'Treat me, don't beat me'* (Kadushin, 1999: 58), the supervisee invites the supervisor to help with personal problems, as a way of deflecting criticism or resisting demands. This is a common game, and it works because the supervisor is being invited to return to a role that is familiar and comfortable to her, that of a professional working with a vulnerable client, rather than the manager and supervisor of a fellow professional. (It's also flattering, as Kadushin notes, to be asked for help.)

Another game, *'Evaluation is not for friends'* (Kadushin, 1999: 59), encourages the supervisor to look at the relationship between supervisor and supervisee as a friendship, rather than a professional or line management relationship. It is particularly easy to fall into this, of course, if, as sometimes happens, the supervisor and supervisee really are friends outside of work, or are former colleagues from the days when the supervisor was also simply a practitioner.

Reducing power disparity

These games reduce the authority of the supervisor in various ways. In the game called *'If you knew Dostoyevsky like I know Dostoyevsky'* (Kadushin, 1999: 59), the supervisee lets it be known that she is much better-informed than the supervisor, and the supervisor feels pressured to fall in with what the supervisee is suggesting rather than have to admit she doesn't know what she is talking about. A similar game is *'So what do you know about it?'* in which the supervisee draws attention to her considerably greater experience, either at work, or at some aspect of life which is relevant to the case under discussion. The supervisor can then end up being instructed by the supervisee and, with roles reversed, the authority of the supervisor is reduced.

Controlling the situation

These are games in which the supervisee finds ways of taking charge of the agenda. In the game *'I have a little list'* (Kadushin, 1999: 60) the supervisee comes to the meeting with a list of questions that she knows the supervisor will enjoy answering. In *'Heading them off at the pass'* (1999: 61) the supervisee is aware that some of his recent practice has been poor, so before the supervisor can criticise him, he launches into ferocious self-criticism:

> There is no failing ... which he does not freely confess in advance, flagellating himself to excess. The supervisor, faced with overwhelming self-derogation, has little option but to reassure the supervisee sympathetically. [This] not only makes difficult an extended discussion of mistakes in the work at the supervisor's initiative, it elicits praise by the supervisor for whatever strengths the supervisee has manifested, however limited. The supervisor, once again, acts out of concern with the troubled, out of his predisposition to comfort the discomforted, out of pleasure in acting the good, forgiving parent. (1999: 61)

Of course, these aren't the only games that supervisees play – Kadushin suggests several more, and you can probably think of others he doesn't mention – but they are certainly all games that I recall from my own experience as a supervisor. Kadushin's point is that games work because they are seductive. They give pleasure and reassurance to the supervisor which she will miss out on if she refuses to play:

> For instance, in declining to go along with ... 'Two Against the Agency', the supervisor has to be comfortable in exercising her administrative authority, willing to risk and deal with supervisee hostility and rejection, and willing to accept the accusation that she is bureaucratically (rather than professionally) orientated. In declining other games, the supervisor denies him- or herself the sweet fruits of flattery, the joys of omniscience, the pleasures of acting as therapist, and the gratification of being well liked. (1999: 63)

RESISTING SUPERVISEE GAMES

However, if we are seduced by the game, we are put in a position where we are no longer able to fully function either as a professional supervisor or as an effective line manager. So it's important to recognise the game being played and resist its temptations. To achieve this we have to do without all those agreeable pleasures and reassurances and, as Carolyn Cousins puts it, 'be aware of the game, but refuse to accommodate its intentions – that is, assertively returning to the performance issues, despite the game' (Cousins, 2010: 288). For example, if the supervisee says, 'You're the best supervisor I've ever had', you might say 'That's nice of you, but, returning to the problem of your recording, I need to see up to date records on this case by the end of next week.'

Sometimes it may be appropriate to actually point out the game. 'This may include going so far as to be explicit about the games by naming them … [something that] needs to be undertaken with understanding of the reasons behind the games and the anxieties of the worker they expose' (Cousins, 2010: 287). The supervisor, might say, for instance, 'It seems to me that whenever I ask you to get your recording up to date, you try and get me to gang up with you against the agency and agree with you that recording isn't important for real practitioners. I have to say that I *don't* agree with you.' Kadushin observes that open confrontation of a game goes against the normal rules of social interaction in which 'each person accepts the line put out by the other person' (1999: 64). This feels uncomfortable, but then again much of what human service professionals do – questioning people's parenting, asking people about whether they can use the toilet – goes against the normal rules of social interaction. Professionalism does mean acting differently from how we act in other contexts.

And, as Kadushin points out, not only do supervisee games, if unchecked, prevent supervisors from doing their job, but they also prevent supervisees from getting the supervision they really need, and so, in that sense, are counterproductive even for the player.

EXERCISE 7.2

Your experience of supervisee games

1. Whether or not you are currently supervising other staff, think about yourself as a supervisee and try and identify some of the games you play, or have played, in order to get your supervisor to do what you want.
2. If you are a supervisor, have you noticed your supervisees playing any of the games I've just discussed? (Or if not those games, then others.) Which games do you find hardest to resist and why?
3. If you're not a supervisor, which games do you think you'd find hardest to resist if you were one? Possibly service users have played similar games with you: 'You are the best social worker I've ever had!' for instance, is a not an uncommon example of a service user playing '*Be nice to me because I am nice to you*'. 'All of the others make me feel like I'm just a number, but you really seem to care', is similar to '*Two against the agency*'. (This is not to say that these things are necessarily said in an entirely manipulative spirit, of course, or that there might not be some truth in them.)

Obviously I don't know what games you've picked, but the question 'Which games do you find hardest to resist and why?' is, I suggest, worth giving some careful thought to. Games that we find hard to resist reveal areas of vulnerability in our professionalism, like chinks in a knight's armour. For instance, people who are not very sure of themselves are vulnerable to flattery because it is reassuring. People who have just moved into management and worry that they are no longer seen as 'one of us' by former colleagues, may be vulnerable to *'Two against the agency'* or to a related but more aggressive game which Kadushin (1999: 60) calls *'All or nothing at all'* in which the supervisee aims to make the supervisor feel that she's sold out by going over to management, and invites her to prove that her loyalties are still with the service users and the front-line staff. If we know where the chinks are in our professional armour, we will be better prepared to deal with attempts to get through them.

GAMES SUPERVISORS PLAY

Kadushin talks about supervisor games also, but in less detail than supervisee games, so my three categories this time do not come from him. The first two (games of 'abdication' and of 'power') are from Lilian Hawthorne (1975), the third ('games of projection and manipulation') is my own. Just like supervisee games they are played by the supervisor to get something she wants or to avoid something she finds uncomfortable. Something to notice is the way these games connect up with supervisee games.

Games of abdication

These are played by supervisors who feel uncomfortable about being in a position of authority over practitioners, and wish to minimise the gap between themselves and their supervisees so as to make the relationship feel as much as possible like one of equals. They may be played by supervisors who are new to the role, or not confident in it. They may also be played by supervisors whose personal drivers include a strong need to please people and be liked (see Chapter 4, p 58ff). Being the manager of a team can be lonely, and we may play these games too when we are missing the feeling of simply being a team member. Similar games are being played by the 'down-with-the-kids' teacher who wants his pupils to feel he is one of them, or by the social worker who conveys to her clients that she would give them everything they wanted if it wasn't for her heartless managers and the heartless 'system'.

Carolyn Cousins (2010: 286) suggests that social workers receive very little help with the transition to management and that, as a result, the shift 'often brings about internal conflicts for the social worker who has seen himself as committed to social justice and "championing the cause of the underdog"'. She goes on to suggest that 'this possibly unconscious, and most likely unspoken, conflict can play itself out in seeking opportunities to prove to others one is still caring, has not forgotten one's roots ... is still challenging authority' (2010: 286).

One very common game is *'I'm really one of you'* in which 'the supervisor blindly supports almost all complaints against higher management from the supervisees, failing to acknowledge they are actually part of management themselves' (Delano and Shah, 2006: 37). Another game is *'They won't let me'* (Hawthorne, 1975: 180), in which (just like the social worker I mentioned a couple of paragraphs ago) the supervisor implies she would like to agree to something, but her hands are tied by more senior managers. A supervisor whose needs make her prone to such games will be *extremely* vulnerable to supervisee games such as *'Two against the system'*, or *'All or nothing at all'*, in which the supervisee is in effect inviting her to prove that she is indeed 'one of you'.

Another abdication game which most supervisors seem to own up to having played at least once is what Delano and Shah call *'Carpet bombing'* (2011: 178). Here, rather than taking up a matter individually with the team member concerned, you issue a general request to the whole team. For instance, rather than confronting a supervisee who is frequently late for work, you send an email to all of your supervisees reminding them to come in on time. This avoids a difficult confrontation with the person concerned – always uncomfortable for a supervisor who is not at ease with her authority – but it is likely to cause resentment among those who are careful to be punctual. It is also very unlikely to work, as very little real pressure has been put on the actual late arriver.

(Perhaps one reason the late arriver is hard to confront is that she is a skilful player of *'Two against the agency'*? 'I'm sure you agree that rigid coming-in times are for bureaucrats,' she might say. 'What really matters after all, is that the service users get the help they need.')

Games of power

Games of abdication are characteristic of the 'permissive' and 'neglectful' corners of the 'parenting styles' quadrant discussed in Chapter 4 (see p 55ff). Games of power, on the other hand, are characteristic of the 'authoritarian' corner. Although they seem very different, games of power do also reflect insecurity on the part of the supervisor about her own authority. It's just that in this case she tries to fend off the insecurity, not by 'getting down with the kids' but by trying to bolster up her power against any challenge. In *'Remember who's boss'*, for instance, 'the supervisor's role is defined as absolute authority and permits no challenges and few choices about decisions in their unit' (Delano and Shah, 2006: 37).

In *'I'm only trying to help you'*, the supervisor exercises control 'in the guise of help' (Hawthorne, 1975: 181), something I fear that human service professions quite often do to their clients also. Kadushin identifies another game called *'I wonder why you said that?*' which might be played by a supervisor made uncomfortable by a supervisee questioning something he said:

> This is the game of redefining honest disagreement so that it appears to be psychological resistance. Honest disagreement requires that the supervisor defend his point of view ... [but] if honest disagreement is defined as resistance, the burden is shifted to the supervisee. He has to examine his needs and motives that prompt him to question what the supervisor has said. (1999: 62)

In another Kadushin game, '*One good question deserves another*' (1999: 62), the supervisor deflects a question which he is not sure how to answer, by putting another question back to the supervisee. In all of these games, the supervisor is ostensibly supporting his supervisee but in fact undermining her to ensure that she doesn't in any way threaten the supervisor's position of superior knowledge and power. Put this way, it sounds almost sinister, but I think we probably all play these games from time to time. I think for instance of a practice teacher attempting to play one or other of these games when made to feel small by an able student who asks awkward questions about 'Why do we do things this way?' and whose knowledge feels much more up to date than her own.

Often of course the games don't achieve the desired effect. We can be more transparent than we think, and the game may be completely obvious to the supervisee!

Games of projection and manipulation

Supervisors have more things than their own power to worry about. One of the day-to-day issues that many supervisors are grappling with is that there is a lot of work coming in that needs allocating and only a limited number of people to do it, some of whom may not be very experienced. This, I've found, can cause a lot of anxiety since it involves either sitting on unallocated work, or allocating work to people who are already very busy, and may not be able to do it very well.

The supervisor may be tempted in these circumstances to project qualities onto supervisees that they don't really possess – for example by overestimating a supervisee's ability to handle an additional case – or to reward supervisees who reduce the supervisor's anxieties by taking on work and claiming to be on top of things: '*I wish the others were as helpful as you*'. Supervisors may engage in other games that play into the more specific needs and drivers of their supervisees in order to get them to take on work. '*It just seemed perfect for you!*' flatters the supervisee's professional skills and therefore makes it difficult to say no.

Another game, '*Don't tell me you've got too much to do, and I won't ask about the corners you're cutting*', played implicitly rather than being expressed out loud, may reduce the anxiety of supervisor and supervisee, but actually undermines the fundamental purpose of supervision by breaking the chain of accountability. *'I'll leave the details to you'*, can be a way of dealing with the fact that the supervisor does not know herself how the supervisee can manage the work she's just given her.

EXERCISE 7.3

Recognising supervisor games

What games have you noticed your own supervisor playing, either now or in the past? (They don't have to be games I've mentioned above.) Why do you think your supervisor plays them?

If you're a supervisor, what games do you play? Why do you play them?

If you're not a supervisor, do you play any games like these with your service users? (Games of abdication? Games of power? Games of projection and manipulation?) If so, why do you do it?

How easy would it be to challenge your supervisor's games?

How easy (if you're a supervisor) would it be to rein in your own?

RESISTING SUPERVISOR GAMES

For a supervisee to challenge the games of her supervisor is *far* more difficult than the other way round, because of the power difference. How do you tell your practice educator that you feel undermined by him, when you know he can pass or fail your placement? How does a newly qualified worker ask for more supervision during her probationary period, when her supervisor could conclude she wasn't up to the job?

In extreme cases, the supervisee may need to appeal to a third party – the student to her university tutor, the newly qualified worker to a more senior manager – but in many cases supervisor games do not amount to serious misconduct and may well be completely unconscious. How do you handle them then?

In fact, precisely because the supervisee is in a relatively vulnerable position in this respect, supervisors have a *huge* responsibility to be honest with themselves about the games they are playing and ensure that they don't inadvertently behave in ways that are destructive to their supervisees' confidence, growth and ability to practise safely. Basically you as a supervisor have to acknowledge the need, or the fear, or the driver, that makes you prone to certain games, and try and push through it. For instance, if you are aware that your student is more able than you are, and seems to know a lot more theory, you would not be human if this didn't make you feel a little insecure. But it actually isn't essential to know more than your student about everything in order to be a helpful practice teacher, and if you remind yourself of this, you may be better able to resist the temptation to play games intended to defend your status – and you will also be better placed to recognise, and not respond to, any games the student plays.

The onus must be on the supervisor to avoid unhelpful games, but there are still things that the supervisee can do as well:

- Don't play along.
- Raise the problems the game is causing in a way that recognises the vulnerability behind the game: 'I really appreciate all your knowledge and practice experience, but I feel you're letting me rely on it too much, and I'm worried I'm not learning to think for myself.'
- Avoid playing supervisee games that will trigger supervisor games. If you play *'If you knew Dostoyevsky like I know Dostoyevsky'* or *'So what do you know about it?'* (even if in only mild and subtle ways) you should not be surprised if your supervisor starts to feel a bit defensive. We might like to have a supervisor who has no insecurities and can cope with anything, but we do have to settle for the fact that our supervisor is only a flawed human being.
- Be specific about what you want, while avoiding being unnecessarily critical of what you've been given up to now. 'I would really like your thoughts on how my thinking is developing. I was wondering, would it be possible for me sometimes to lay out all my thoughts on a case without any interruptions and then for you to give me your feedback?' would probably work better than, 'I wish just once you would shut up and let me tell you what I think before you butt in!'
- Of course, there is always the option of being assertive, naming the game, and asking for it to stop. I am simply acknowledging here that this can be difficult when the supervisor is your boss.

GAMES SUPERVISORS AND SUPERVISEES PLAY TOGETHER

All of the supervisee games I have described are in a sense played together, since they require the participation of the supervisor to work. (Things are a little different with supervisor games because of the power difference.) However, there are certain games which are characteristically a joint effort. Figure 7.1 illustrates a kind of game that supervisors and supervisees can play together to help each other manage their anxieties. It is of course a very dangerous game!

What we are talking about here is a form of groupthink (see Chapter 5, p 88), in which this little group of two, the supervisor and the supervisee, tacitly agree to

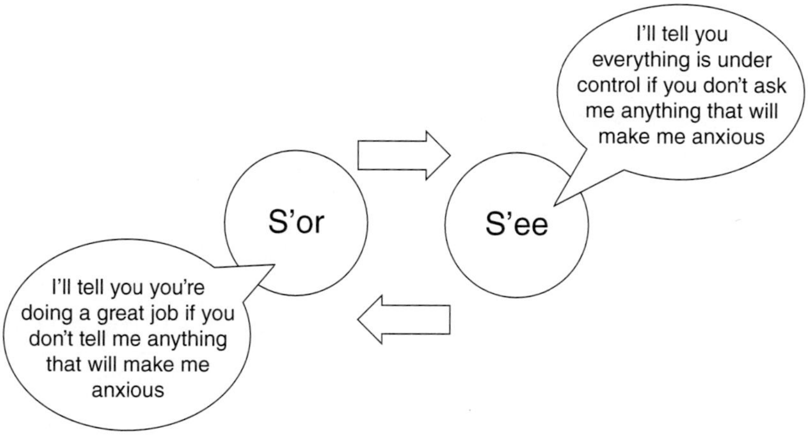

Figure 7.1 I'll tell you what you want to hear if you tell me what I want to hear (supervisor/supervisee game)

bolster one another's precarious sense of security by protecting each other from discordant messages. These kinds of cosy and collusive games can quite easily build up in a supervision session.

One of the characteristics of groupthink is a tendency of the group to work together to discount evidence that the group consensus might be wrong. This can manifest itself in, among other things, a combined effort to dismiss the views of another professional: *'She's always pushing the panic button', 'He just wants us to be involved so he doesn't have to take responsibility himself'* etc. I think this dangerous cosiness can be tackled to some extent by naming it: 'Are we getting a bit complacent here?' 'She [the panicky professional] may be a pain sometimes but we probably ought to think about what she says all the same, and make sure we're not dismissing her too readily'.

The risk of this sort of unprofessional cosiness building up will be reduced in any case if both supervisor and supervisee have been careful to avoid games that have the effect of blurring the boundaries of the supervisor/supervisee relationship.

CONCLUDING NOTES FOR SUPERVISORS AND SUPERVISEES

Notes for supervisors (including practice educators)

The supervisor games you play and the supervisee games you're susceptible to will both come from the same place. I've suggested we all have 'chinks in our armour'

(Continued)

which we need to be aware of in order to have the best possible working relationship with supervisees.

It's an important insight that resisting games means denying ourselves pleasures and reassurances that we seek. It can be hard to do this in a job where you are beset with other difficult things to deal with, and comfort and reassurance may be in short supply. But you will become a more valuable and effective supervisor if you do so, and this will bring its own rewards.

While it's very important to recognise, and not play along with, supervisee games, it's possibly even more important not to play games yourself, because the power advantage you have means that it is much more difficult for supervisees to challenge supervisor's games than vice versa.

All of this is really about *owning* the job you have. This can be challenging at first for people who have moved from practice into management. However, you have almost certainly had to make a similar transition in the past when you first trained and qualified and had to learn to act as a professional when with service users, and not just as a friend.

Notes for supervisees (including students on placement)

In the process of writing this chapter, it has struck me that what it has really been about is grown-up, professional communication, as opposed to immature and boundaryless communication.

You have some responsibility to try not to play supervisee games with your supervisor, even if he or she is susceptible to them.

But what is difficult for supervisees is dealing with supervisor games. As I've noted, you may be able to handle some of these yourself, by being tactful and recognising the needs that lie behind them, but the power difference makes it difficult. However, even just recognising them, will reduce their impact.

CHAPTER SUMMARY

This chapter has looked at ways in which game-playing by either or both parties can occur in supervision.

Having looked at the concept of 'games' (in the sense used by Eric Berne), I looked at games played by supervisees with the aim of 'manipulating demand', 'redefining the relationship', 'reducing the power disparity' or 'controlling the situation' (the categories were from Kadushin, 1999). I discussed how each game works because it rewards the supervisor in some way for playing along. And I discussed ways in which supervisors can resist supervisee games.

Supervisors also play games and I grouped these under 'games of abdication' (in which the supervisor avoids owning her own authority), 'games of power' (in which the supervisor jealously guards her power), and 'games of projection and manipulation' which the supervisor uses to get people to do things and to fend off information that would make her anxious. Again, I discussed how supervisees might resist these games while acknowledging that the supervisor has more power.

Finally, I discussed various collusive games, akin to groupthink (discussed in Chapter 5) that the supervisor and supervisee might play together, and suggested ways to avoid these also.

8

THE FRAMEWORK

CONTENTS

In the last three chapters, I have focused on supervision in terms of processes that go on within the supervision session. (In Chapters 5 and 6 I was looking at what needs to happen in supervision in order for the supervisor to get a sense of what is really going on, and add real value to casework. In Chapter 7, I looked at some of the interpersonal processes that may get in the way of that.) In this chapter I'm coming back to the wider context within which supervision takes place.

MEDIATION, SUPPORT AND DEVELOPMENT

As part of that wider context, I want to say a little more about some of the functions of a supervisor which I have discussed relatively little up to now. In Chapter 2, I borrowed the idea of functions from Jane Wonnacott (2012), who gives four functions: Management, Development, Support and Mediation. I suggested a fifth function – Wonnacott doesn't give it a separate name – which I called Clarification. One way or another, this book has had a fair amount to say so far about Clarification and about aspects of Support and Management, but I have said comparatively little about Mediation or Development, and there are *aspects* of Support which I haven't discussed very much at all.

Mediation

The mediation function of supervision is about sitting between practitioners and senior management and trying to help both sides understand each other's needs: it's something that happens both within supervision sessions and in other wider settings, such as team meetings, within which supervisors (whether they are managers, senior practitioners or practice educators) typically interact with supervisees.

Some supervisors are better at the top down side of this communication, others are better at bottom up, some may not be very strong on communicating either way, and some achieve the balance required to communicate well in both directions. Table 8.1 illustrates some different styles of mediation. You may see some connections between the various styles and some of the 'games' discussed in Chapter 7 ('Bottom Up' mediators, for instance, are likely to play *'I'm really one of you'* [p 121], 'Top Down' mediators are likely to be prone to 'games of power' [p 121]). I would argue that only the balanced style really *is* mediation in the true sense of acting as a facilitator of communication between two or more parties, rather than being an advocate for one or other of them.

Being a genuine mediator can be uncomfortable for a supervisor because if you maintain that balanced position, you are likely to become aware at times that both your supervisees and your bosses would like more from you than you are prepared to give. You will have to resist games such as *'Two against the agency'* and *'All or nothing at all'*

Table 8.1 Mediation styles

	Loyalties and priorities	Characteristics of the style
Top Down mediation style	*Keen to prove yourself to senior management.* *Loyalties go upwards more than downwards.*	• Strong commitment to driving through changes requested by senior management. • Less strong on passing messages up to senior management that senior managers may not want to hear. • One sided.
Bottom Up mediation style	*Keen to prove to staff that you are still on their side.* *Loyalties go downwards more than upwards.*	• Strong on letting senior management know about the challenges faced by your staff. • See yourself battling the system on behalf of your staff: An advocate for front-line staff. • Not strong on implementing changes that your staff will not like. • One sided but in the opposite way to Top Down.
Minimalist mediation style	*Not keen in getting involved in communication in either direction.* *No strong loyalties or commitments.*	• Not strong on mediation at all. • Will do what is necessary in order to avoid trouble. Most likely this will involve superficial compliance with Top Down requests.
Balanced mediation style	*Recognises that for the organisation to function, the centre of the organisation and its staff need to understand each other's needs.* *Engaged with the organisation, but tries to avoid taking sides.*	• Communicates changes required by senior management clearly, and without undermining them, but in a way that is sensitive to how staff are likely to feel. • Communicates needs and concerns of staff upwards, but in a way that recognises senior management needs. • Mediation in the true sense of trying to facilitate communication between both sides.

from supervisees who think you should be a more whole-hearted advocate for them, but you will also have to resist similar pressures from senior managers playing a game which might be called *'Have you really got what it takes?'*, *'The right stuff'* or *'If you can't stand the heat …'*. Top down senior managers tend to see themselves as tough people, taking the hard decisions which people lower down the hierarchy would rather not have to face, and then having the guts to drive them through. (The macho aspect of all this is not, I suspect, entirely unrelated to the fact that, while human service agencies are staffed predominantly by women, the percentage of men increases steadily the further up the hierarchy you go.) When I became a team manager, I remember being explicitly told by my own manager that he expected my loyalties to be upward from now on. (I don't think he was right, as will be apparent, but I don't think my loyalties should have been purely downward either.)

The idea that managers have to implement tough decisions which front-line staff would rather not face does, however, contain more than a little truth. For instance, if the government cuts an agency's budget, management has to implement those cuts somehow, even if front-line staff are reluctant to accept that reality. But to assume that *all* resistance to management directives is simply the result of people burying their heads in the sand and refusing to face reality is simplistic and rather self-serving (rather like blaming service users for not wanting the service you are offering by describing them as 'unwilling to engage'). This one-sided view has, unfortunately, sometimes been actively encouraged by the literature on change management which many senior managers will have imbued on courses:

> Studies of change appear to take the perspective, or bias, of those seeking to bring about change, in which it is presumed that change agents are doing the right and proper things while change recipients throw up unreasonable obstacles or barriers. (Ford et al., 2008: 362)

A more grown-up and balanced take is that, yes, sometimes people do resist innovations simply because they are uncomfortable with change, or are unwilling to face political and practical realities, but these aren't the *only* reasons they resist. Sometimes they resist because of the *way* that change is imposed:

> People are not simply and naturally resistant to change. What comes closer to a universal truth about human behavior is that people resist the *imposition of change* ... When one's feeling of freedom is in jeopardy, the immediate reaction is likely to be an attempt to regain the feeling of freedom ... The degree of ease and success with which an organizational change is introduced is therefore directly proportional to the amount of choice that people feel they have in determining and implementing the change. (Burke, 2011: 109. My italics)

An imposed change feels like a loss of control, in a service where there are already many troubling things that make you anxious because you can't control them. And this is particularly so in an environment of low trust. Myers et al. point out that 'Trust is an important factor in successful change because voluntary change involves vulnerability' (2012: 97). To build trust you need communication in order to allow people to feel that they are being listened to, and that they are being told what is really going on. (This advice is equally applicable to casework with involuntary service users.)

Sometimes, too, people resist changes because they know the realities of their job better than senior managers and they genuinely believe that some aspects of what is proposed *just won't work*. And, to be fair, they are often right! A lot of attempted organisational changes do not turn out as planned – *most* of them, in fact, according to the American change management guru, John Kotter (2007). But the point here is not that front-line staff 'know better' than senior managers. That would clearly be nonsense: senior managers know about a *lot* of things that front-line staff don't even have to think about. The real point is that the reverse is also true: front-line staff know a lot of things that senior managers don't know or have forgotten, and senior managers would do well to take some of this knowledge on board if they want their plans to be a success. So resistance is not necessarily bad for the change process if it involves feeding back information that may help avoid problems. The *assumption* that resistance is necessarily bad can lead to the leaders of change missing 'its potential contribution of increasing the likelihood of successful implementation' (Ford et al., 2008: 363).

So two-way communication is important for any organisation both in terms of maintaining trust, and also so as to ensure that the organisation as a whole is making decisions on the basis of information that is as complete and accurate as possible. Supervisors of front-line staff are sandwiched, sometimes rather uncomfortably, between practice and management, and it can be tempting to take one 'side' or another. But the truth is that their unique 'middle' position (see Sims, 2003, for more on this) is vital in itself, and that, rather than taking sides, middles are most useful when they act as a channel of communication between both 'sides' on the basis that each has something to tell the other. Such a stance, is, I think, consistent with the *authoritative* position which I discussed in Chapter 4. The authoritative school teacher, who respects, listens to and encourages her pupils, but does not play the '*I'm really one of you*' game of ganging up with them against the 'system', is refusing to take sides in exactly the way that I am recommending here.

I've talked about this so far by looking at the recurring issue of organisational change, something that is almost always unpopular with front-line staff, who understandably prefer to maintain the stability that allows them to get on with the job. However, the mediation role isn't confined to change management. Supervisors may also have to mediate on issues to do with resources, for instance. (Here, senior management control the purse strings, and are aware of the many demands on the budget, while practitioners are aware, in a way that senior managers are not, of the actual lives of real service users and the day-to-day implications of their needs.) Another issue where mediation might be needed is in connection with recording systems. Elaborate recording systems often seem excessive to practitioners because they do not seem to have any obvious benefit for service users and take time away from direct practice. (I gave an example in the previous chapter of a supervisee making just this argument.) However, they may be important for senior managers who need data to satisfy inspectors, or to make out the case for additional resources from central government. These are all situations in which the supervisor could take one side or another but will usually be most useful by trying to mediate in a balanced way, explaining the needs of each side to the other and seeking a way forward that both can live with.

EXERCISE 8.1

Mediation styles – your own experience

1 Look at the four mediation styles I set out in Table 8.1, and ask yourself firstly which one most accurately describes your current line manager, supervisor, or practice teacher, and which styles seem most characteristic of managers or supervisors you've had in the past. How would you describe the experience of having a line manager or supervisor with that particular style in terms of your relationship with the rest of the organisation? You might look at questions like whether or not it engendered a feeling of trust, whether it allowed you to feel heard, and whether it challenged you to take on board the decisions of senior management in a positive way.
2 If you are supervising others how would you describe yourself in terms of mediation style? Having identified your style, why do you think that your style is like that?

I'd suggest that our mediation style depends on how confident we are at holding an autonomous line, and the degree to which we feel we need the safety of a larger group to give our allegiance to. It also, let us be frank, may depend on our perception of self-interest career-wise, since a 'top down' approach is likely to win the approval of managers above you in the hierarchy. I suggest though, that a courteous but assertive 'balanced' approach need not alienate senior managers and may win more respect in the long run. 'Bottom up' and 'minimalist' styles, on the other hand, are unlikely to be seen in a positive light.

Support

The kind of careful supervision that was discussed in Chapters 5 and 6 will usually be experienced as supportive by supervisees, since it helps them with the anxious business of interpreting what they have seen, and making decisions. Support is not the *only* function it performs. This kind of supervision is also important for line management accountability, and it is central to the additional function I called 'clarification', whose purpose is not about making staff feel supported, but about maximising the quality of the response to service users. Nevertheless, meticulous supervision which provides space for reflection and analysis will go a long way towards making staff feel supported.

But there is another kind of support that supervisors provide which I have discussed very little in the book so far, other than briefly introduce the term 'restorative function' (after Proctor, 1988) in Chapter 2 to describe it. The work of most human service professionals involves not only stress (the normal work pressures that are found in many jobs), but also *distress*, in the form of frequent exposure to matters that most people prefer not to think about too much at all, such as illness, death, bereavement, self-harm and child abuse. Human service professionals are also frequently involved in performing tasks which most people would hate to have anything to do with, such as detaining a distressed individual in a mental hospital, or removing a child from a neglectful family. (I recall seeing a very experienced social worker returning to the office after removing a new-born baby from a mother: he just sat at his desk and wept.) And of course human service professionals, like everyone else, have problems in their lives outside that may affect their work. Part of the support function of supervision is to look after supervisees, check how they are coping, address any problems that may be creating difficulties, and allow them opportunities to off-load.

Supervisors walk a difficult line in this regard. They cannot become the counsellor or therapist for a troubled member of staff and they need to be wary of being drawn in to 'games' which place them in such a role. '*Treat me, don't beat me*' (Kadushin, 1999) is one such 'game' that we discussed in the previous chapter (though in practice it may take a less dramatic form on the lines of '*Look after me, don't ask me to take on work*'). Talking to groups of supervisors, I find that it is surprisingly common for them to have one troubled team member who has effectively become a passenger, not just for a short period, but over a very extended period of time. But it is often outside the scope of supervision to solve whatever problem lies behind someone withdrawing from the work in that kind of way. In the event of serious, chronic difficulties, supervisors need to refer that support function on to actual counselling services. (It is important to remember, too, that such scenarios have an impact on the service that the team is supposed to deliver: by allowing one member of a team of ten to become in effect a service user rather than a worker, a team reduces by 10% the resource it has available for its *actual* service users. So the question of the suitability of that individual for the job is a nettle that, sooner or later, has to be grasped. But this is something we'll come back to in Chapter 9.)

Development

Careful supervision, as described in Chapters 5 and 6, in which due space is provided for reflection and analysis, is naturally conducive to staff development, but the development function of supervisors, just like their support function, is not confined to this. There should be a slower rhythm also, stretching over years rather than weeks, which allows professional growth to be recognised, new responsibilities discussed, and training needs considered.

But to look at this slower rhythm, we need to step outside of the supervision cycle and look at the larger cycle of induction and appraisal which will be the subject of the rest of this chapter.

INDUCTION

One year, in the course of my teaching on supervision, I invited a very experienced manager, someone who'd been supervising staff for a quarter of a century, to talk to a group of supervisors about induction of new staff. She told me afterwards that she'd been very struck by how one-sided their approach had been. They were all very keen to show how supportive they were to new staff, and to demonstrate the various ways in which they helped new workers to find their feet and feel at home in their new environment – all of which was of course important – but they were much less strong on setting out their *expectations* of new members of staff. Indeed (she told me) they hardly seemed to have grasped at all that this was a key element of induction. I have to say, I felt that I'd missed this important point myself: in my days as a supervisor, all the training I'd received on induction had emphasised the welcoming, supportive aspect, rather than the 'setting expectations' aspect. And yet she was absolutely right, partly because during the first few months habits are laid down which may be hard to change later, and partly because the first few months are – for everyone concerned, including the new member of staff – by far the best and least painful time to address issues of capability. If someone just is not suitable for the job, whether because they lack the ability, or the temperament, or the interest, it is much better for them and you to identify and address this at the beginning, during the probationary period, than have to deal with this years later, after much struggle and unhappiness, and at great cost to the individual, the team and the service.

Thinking about this reminded me of the parenting styles quadrant (Baumrind, 1978) that I discussed in Chapter 4 (see Figure 4.2 on p 56). The fact that it is a quadrant arises from the fact that there are two distinct dimensions: *responsiveness* and *demandingness*. The supervisors who were keen to demonstrate how careful they were to welcome new team members and help them feel at home, were very aware that they needed to be on the responsive end of the responsiveness dimension – and there is nothing wrong with that! – but they were forgetting altogether the existence of the demandingness dimension, and therefore paying no attention to where they ought to be on it.

EXERCISE 8.2

Induction styles

In the parenting styles quadrant, the four quarters are '*permissive*' (low demandingness/high responsiveness), '*neglectful*' (low demandingness/low responsiveness), '*authoritarian*' (high demandingness/low responsiveness), and '*authoritative*' (high demandingness/high responsiveness). If these were descriptions, not of parenting styles, but of different kinds of induction programme, what would the characteristics of each be?

Which of these describes most accurately the kinds of induction programme you have experienced yourself as a new member of staff (or a student on placement)? If you yourself have organised inductions for new members of staff, which of these describes most accurately your approach?

My own thoughts about the differences between these four approaches are as follows:

- *Permissive induction*: This would be a very gentle introduction to the job with little pressure. There would be lots of information and support provided, but very little set out in the way of demands or expectations. I'm not sure that many people have actually experienced this, but (as noted above) many supervisors seem to feel that something like this is what they *should* aspire to. As I've already indicated, I now think this is a mistake. A new member of staff needs to be clear on boundaries and expectations, without which it is difficult to know what the job is supposed to entail. Unless such expectations have been set out clearly, it will be difficult to know later whether the member of staff has shown herself capable of meeting them.
- *Neglectful induction*: This is when new staff are more or less given a pile of cases and left to get on with it, without much guidance or information, but also without expectations being clearly spelled out. Many people seem to have experienced something approaching this, and the emphasis that my students placed on a very welcoming and supportive approach was often based on a desire not to repeat this mistake (much as over-indulgent parents are sometimes trying not to repeat the mistakes of their own neglectful or abusive parents). Again, the absence of clear expectations makes it difficult for the staff member to know what is the standard of work expected of them, and difficult for the organisation to assess the staff member's progress. The absence of support will also mean that any progress is slow, and that poor working habits may develop unnoticed.
- *Authoritarian induction*: If you have seen the film *An Officer and a Gentleman*, a fine example of an authoritarian induction is provided by the character Sergeant Emil Foley, as played by Louis Gossett Jr. As he prepares his group of newly recruited naval aviators for their careers, Sgt Foley is extremely demanding and almost completely unresponsive, constantly asking more of them, repeatedly telling them in the bluntest possible terms that their performance isn't adequate, and allowing no space whatsoever for weakness or vulnerability. (If you haven't seen that particular film, similar regimes can

be seen in almost any film that deals with the induction of newly recruited soldiers: how true to life they are, I'm not in a position to say.) Arguably a tough approach to induction is justified in the armed forces where new recruits must be prepared for situations where an enemy is trying to kill you and will make absolutely no allowances for weakness, but new military recruits pay a high price for this, and they can and do crack tragically under the strain (see, for instance BBC, 2018). I doubt whether any reader has experienced anything this extreme in human services, although some induction programmes may be experienced as being quite demanding and not very supportive. While I certainly do *not* advocate Sgt Foley's approach to induction, I think it is important to recognise that demandingness has its place. Ours is difficult, challenging work, and (as with military recruits) there is no point in shielding new staff from this fact during their probationary period when their suitability for the job is still under review.

- *Authoritative induction*: Since I advocated an authoritative approach in Chapter 4, and a 'balanced' approach to mediation earlier in this chapter, the reader won't be surprised to learn that I am arguing here for an authoritative approach to induction. This is a demanding approach too, and one which sets challenging expectations in terms of the standard and pace of work, but at the same time ensures that support is available, both in the form of good, regular, in-depth supervision and in terms of other arrangements, such as mentoring, induction packs and so on.

Figure 8.1 summarises the above. A key point is that the two 'high demand' styles ('*authoritative*' and '*authoritarian*') have the great advantage of setting out expectations, so that the new member of staff knows what standard of work is expected. These then provide a benchmark against which progress can be measured and problems identified during the probationary period. However, the *authoritative* approach, which is responsive as well as demanding, is much more likely to actually help someone to *meet* those high expectations, since a human service job requires the development of skills that can only be learned through in-depth human interaction.

THE SUPERVISION AGREEMENT

The supervision agreement should be a component of any induction package. Supervision is going to be the means by which staff development is both assessed and supported, and it is essential that new staff understand from the beginning what is expected of them in supervision sessions, and what they can expect. It should not be assumed that people already know what supervision is. I suspect that, if you asked

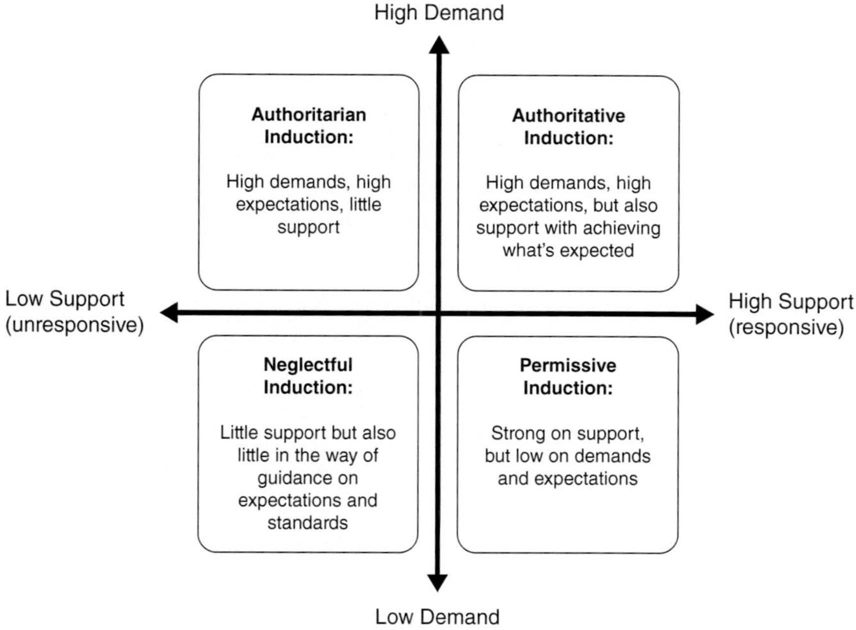

Figure 8.1 Induction styles (based on Baumrind's parenting styles)

members of the public to say what 'supervision' consisted of, they would probably describe what, in Chapter 1, I referred to as accountability supervision, and might not think at all of what I referred to as clinical supervision. New supervisees, and particularly students on placement, may well make that same assumption, though they may have other assumptions of their own based on hearsay or previous experiences. In any case, it is not safe to assume that they just *know*! And yet, during my training and at the beginning of my career, I don't recall anyone spelling out for me what I needed to bring to supervision and what I should expect. (Nor, I am sorry to say, do I recall having that conversation with new supervisees when I was a supervisor.)

Many agencies have standard proformas for supervision agreements and, if those are a requirement, clearly you will have to use them. From what I have seen of them, they are often strong on important practical details. So, for instance, supervisors commit themselves to make available a regular, uninterrupted timeslot in a venue which ensures some privacy, supervisees commit themselves to being punctual, keeping the time free and preparing for agreed agenda items. However, my impression is that they are sometimes less strong on setting out what each party should expect of the other in relation to the *content* of supervision. Given that supervisees do not necessarily know what they ought to be able to expect, or what they themselves ought to share, in supervision, I suggest that it is useful to be explicit about the nature of the supervision cycle and the fact that it includes Reflection and Analysis.

Reflection

I do not think it is necessarily obvious to everyone that it is appropriate to discuss one's own feelings in supervision, for in many jobs it wouldn't usually be appropriate to discuss them. (I think of the *An Officer and a Gentleman* military training regime I discussed above: talking about feelings would not go down well in that context. Even, say, a bank manager would probably not want to be given an account of the feelings of staff as a matter of course.) In human services, though, for all the reasons discussed in Chapter 5, acknowledging one's own feelings is often necessary to an understanding of the case.

But I do not think that simply including a phrase like 'I agree to be open about my feelings' in a learning agreement is likely to make much difference unless it is accompanied by some explanation of why feelings are important, and also some reassurance that negative feelings such as fear or anger will not in themselves be taken as evidence of unsuitability for practice. It might be helpful to share the fact that fear and anger are normal, and have often been experienced by the supervisor herself.

Analysis

Some supervisees may come to supervision, I suspect, with the expectation that 'I tell her what's happened, and she tells me what to do', or 'I tell her what I think I should do, and she tells me whether that's OK or not'. These might indeed be the expectations of supervisors in other kinds of organisations. And of course both of these *will* happen in supervision – it is not necessarily practicable to engage in very detailed exploration of every single case. However, I suggest that it is important to open up the idea of *analysis* as being a part of supervision, and make clear to supervisees that there is an expectation that facts, impressions and gut feelings will be explored by supervisor and supervisee together in supervision to arrive at some of kind of interpretation that can be used as the basis of action. I know when I began work as a social worker I was for some time under the impression that I *ought* to be able to understand what was going on in a case, and that, just by thinking about it, I *ought* to know what to do. It would be helpful to have had it explained to me that uncertainty is normal, and even inevitable, but that by openly sharing and comparing ideas, it becomes a little less daunting and impenetrable.

Laying the groundwork

What I am really suggesting here is that, as with other aspects of supervision, clarity at the beginning about the content of supervision provides a good foundation for a productive working relationship over time. Confusion and lack of clarity at the beginning, on the other hand, is likely to store up problems and misunderstandings.

Exactly the same is true, of course, of casework relationships with service users. By establishing a shared understanding of the working relationship from the beginning, a supervisor is not only laying the ground for productive supervision, she is also modelling good casework practice.

EXERCISE 8.3

Supervision agreements

1 From the perspective of yourself as a new and inexperienced supervisee (or indeed a student on placement): What was your own experience of the beginning of your first supervisory relationships? Was the supervisor explicit with you about what to expect? Were you clear what supervision was? Were you left with doubts, uncertainties or misconceptions?

2 (For current practice educators and supervisors). How have you introduced students/new workers to supervision? Do you think that there may have been some misapprehension on their part as to what supervision was, what it would include, and what it was for?

3 (For supervisees and supervisors, including students and practice educators). Based on your own experience, what in particular do you think needs to be clarified in a supervision agreement?

APPRAISALS

Annual appraisals should ideally also be part of the wider framework within which casework supervision takes place: an opportunity to step back from the hurly-burly of casework, and take stock on the development of the supervisee and her current needs. In my experience, supervisors tend to be rather constrained by appraisal proformas that are very 'top down', in that they are focused on trying to ensure that staff are aligned with the agenda of senior management (for example by setting goals and targets that align with the organisation's current priorities). All of this is perfectly legitimate, of course, but if it became the *sole* focus of appraisals, it would be understandable if staff members did not feel that the exercise was there to meet their needs. One survey of performance appraisals in the public sector in America highlighted the need for 'employees [to] view this as a constructive process rather than simply another management activity' (Seldon and Sowa, 2011: 260), but my impression from talking to supervisors is that those who carry out the appraisals very often do view them as just a 'management activity' to be gone through, rather than a significant moment in the supervisory relationship. Writing about appraisals of doctors, Sue Morrison and Helen Halpern note that the 'formal need to monitor competencies and politically defined targets tended to follow a "tick-box" culture and the more developmental approaches suffered' as a result (2012: 106).

Clearly, if tick-box forms are a requirement of the organisation, they can't simply be ignored, but there is no reason why an appraisal interview should not extend beyond the purely formal aspects to become an opportunity for both supervisee and supervisor to reflect on progress and challenges over the past year. Morrison and Halpern recommend:

- sharing the locus of control between the appraiser and appraisee [*that is: allow both parties to contribute to the agenda*];
- restoring a developmental agenda within a regulatory framework that risks becoming focused on superficial targets and competencies [*that is: retain a wider agenda that focuses on what the individual professional needs at this point in her career, and not just on what the organisation as a whole wants from its staff*];
- helping an appraisee to reflect on his or her professional experience to stimulate the potential for deeper learning [*that is: use open-ended questions to free the appraisee to talk about what has been important for her, and don't just ask questions about performance relative to targets and competencies*];
- encourage reflection on the complex reality of doctors' working lives [*that is: the totality of doctors' working lives, and not just those few aspects that are currently the subject of targets, or lists of competencies*]. (2012: 106. My own additions in italics.)

The point here is that each appraisee is an individual. No two will be at exactly the same point, no two will have exactly the same needs or exactly the same combination of skills and learning needs, and it is extremely unlikely that any one appraisee's current developmental needs will be captured in their entirety by an evaluation of that individual's progress relative to the organisation's current goals. I am certainly not suggesting that the formal framework be ignored, or that the needs of the organisation be disrespected, but rather that the appraiser should open up the process so that it goes beyond what is required by the organisation in order to address the needs of the individual professional. Just as there is more than one stakeholder in supervision (see Chapter 2), there is, or should be, more than one stakeholder in appraisal. And, apart from anything else, the organisation itself will benefit if this is done (as will service users), since it will result in staff who feel supported, and feel that their own development needs are being addressed. Seldon and Sowa note:

> We ... found a significant relationship between perceptions of the performance management process and one's desire to stay with the organization ... Moreover, organizations where staff's perceptions of the performance management system are higher report significantly less voluntary turnover of staff. (2011: 258)

My suggestion then is that, rather than just assess progress against targets and competencies, the appraiser should develop her own set of questions aimed at exploring progress in a more open-ended way which might include some of the following:

- How has this last year been for you?
- What do you feel you've been getting better at?
- What have you been finding difficult?
- What achievements have you felt most proud of?
- What have been the biggest challenges?
- What knowledge or skills do you feel you could do with training on?
- What knowledge or skills do you feel you could share with others?
- Do you still think this is the right job for you at this stage, or is there another job you feel you should be thinking about?

It is also a good opportunity to reflect on the supervisory relationship itself (assuming that the appraiser has been the supervisor also over the year) and address any problems there.

CONCLUDING NOTES FOR SUPERVISORS AND SUPERVISEES

Notes for supervisors (including practice educators)

The point of this chapter has really been that supervision is more than just about talking about cases, or about specific pieces of work, but is about the progress of the supervisee as a professional and as a member of an organisation.

When you are combining 'accountability' supervision with 'clinical' supervision, you need to take seriously the needs of both the supervisee and the organisation, and I have encouraged you to think about your own 'mediation style': the way in which you act as a conduit for information to pass up and down the organisation between its leaders and its practitioners. I've suggested that to really be a mediator, you need to avoid taking 'sides', even if taking sides is the easier thing to do.

I've also invited you to look at induction and appraisal, events that take place outside the ordinary supervision cycle, which address the place of the supervisee in the team and her progress. I've noted that induction, the associated supervision agreement, and appraisal, typically all have to take place within a formal framework defined by the organisation. However, I've suggested that, while you obviously shouldn't ignore your organisation's formal requirements, you can move beyond them, to make all these

(Continued)

processes more meaningful for the individuals concerned, something which is ultimately in the interests of the organisation too.

In the discussion on induction, I particularly emphasised the need to challenge as well as to support, by laying out your expectations. This allows you to address many performance problems early on, when they are relatively easy to deal with for everyone concerned, but also lays a solid foundation for dealing with problems that crop up later. I will come back to this in the next chapter.

Although I did not specifically mention practice educators in this discussion, they are a particularly obvious case in point: better to be clear from an early stage on what is needed to pass the placement, rather than leave the student unaware that her performance is problematic until a late stage.

Notes for supervisees (including students on placement)

You ought to expect to be clear about what supervision is for, when and where it will happen, and what it will consist of. If you are not, then ask!

You ought to expect more from your supervisor than casework supervision. Your supervisor should act as a channel of communication – in both directions – between yourself and the organisation. Your supervisor should also be supporting your career and giving you opportunities to reflect on your progress and your needs.

However, your supervisor is not just there for you. She is also there for the organisation – and indeed for service users – and this is how it should be. You supervisor can and should challenge you, and set her expectations in terms of the standard of work that is required of you.

CHAPTER SUMMARY

This chapter has moved away from the content of regular supervision sessions discussed in previous chapters to look at some of the other tasks of supervisors and supervisees.

It looked at the mediation function of supervisors/managers – their role as a channel of communication between two of the key stakeholders in supervision: the organisation and its professional staff. And I offered a typology of mediation styles. A genuine mediator, I suggested, does not take sides, but attempts to interpret each 'side' to the other.

I then looked at the broader developmental role of supervisors, as they see supervisees through induction and appraisals. In both cases, I argued in favour of a broader interpretation of these events, than a simple, organisation-oriented, tick-box exercise.

In the case of appraisals, I suggested a broader look at staff development than is entailed in simply checking their progress against targets and competency frameworks, though organisational requirements do of course need to be met.

In the case of induction, I suggested that it is useful to think of this in relation to two distinct dimensions. Firstly, there is responsiveness – an induction should welcome new staff and help them adjust as quickly as possible to the working environment – but secondly, there is demandingness. An induction should be clear on expectations of staff in terms of the standard and pace of their work. This is important because the probationary period is by far the best time to address issues of competency and suitability for the job, and because clear expectations need to be there from the beginning, if problems with performance are going to be effectively addressed. The next chapter will look further at these sorts of problems.

9

DEALING WITH PROBLEMS

CONTENTS

This chapter will look at the role of the supervisor when there are problems with the performance of a supervisee that are affecting that staff member's ability to deliver a service, or function as part of the team. Such problems are common. When I teach groups of supervisors, there are always several who report chronic difficulties with particular members of staff, most commonly members of staff who for one reason or another are doing very little work. The chapter is about the role of the supervisor in this. I will therefore not be dealing here with serious disciplinary problems involving unethical behaviour or dangerous practice, which are outside the scope of supervision, and are a matter for the agency's human resources department to manage. In fact any significant performance problem needs to be managed in consultation with human resources, assuming it is not simply a short-term problem that clearly results from temporary circumstances.

EXERCISE 9.1

What am I finding difficult?

(For supervisors). Looking at the people you currently supervise (or have supervised in the past), who if any, presents you (or presented you) with the most difficulties as a supervisor? That is to say, whose performance – or perhaps attitude – are you most worried about? What is your sense of what the rest of your team feel about this person's current contribution to the team and how you are handling it?

(For supervisees). Is there a member of your team who you, or other team members, are finding difficult as a colleague, either because of their attitude to work, or because of the amount of work they are able to do? What is your feeling, or the feeling of other team members, about the way this person is handled by your supervisor?

The last point, about the feelings of the rest of the team, is important to bear in mind. If a supervisor is finding a team member's behaviour or attitude difficult, then it is likely that other team members will find them difficult too, and may well feel that the supervisor should be doing something about it. What is more, a poorly performing human service professional will have a negative impact on the lives of the people she works with. This is not a them/us, management versus staff, issue. As Hugh Constant points out:

> If poor performance is affecting the lives of vulnerable people, then you have to dedicate the effort to putting together a well-evidenced, timely and robust capability process. In the end, that will be in the best interests of you, the team, the team's clients, and even the overwhelmed worker themselves. (Constant, 2017)

PROBLEMS THAT COME UP

Every situation is different, but in my own experience, and on the basis of what I have heard from groups of supervisees, the kinds of difficulties that supervisors commonly encounter can be summed up under the following two headings. I should stress that, while these behaviours I am describing represent real challenges to the supervisor and the rest of the team, this is not to say that the person concerned does not have good reasons for behaving in such a way. They may well feel that the behaviour is not their fault, or is justified under the circumstances. Ultimately there is always a reason.

- *Maverick behaviour:* The supervisee won't accept direction, is resistant to questioning, avoids doing tasks even when specifically asked to complete them, or avoids addressing issues (such as lateness, or uncompleted recording) even when specifically asked to do so. Some such supervisees may play supervision games such as '*Two against the system*', or '*All or nothing at all*' (Kadushin, 1999; see Chapter 7 for explanation), and may feel their behaviour is justified because they know better, or care more, than management. If this supervisee's behaviour is tolerated by the supervisor, this will be resented by other team members who see these colleagues 'being allowed to get away with' behaviour that they would not be allowed to indulge in. However, the team member who behaves in a 'maverick' way may also be admired by some colleagues as a rebel against the system.
- *Underperformance:* The supervisee seems to lack the motivation, the ability or the confidence (or likely some combination of these) to work to the standard that might be expected of someone in her job. She may resist taking on the amount of work that would be expected of other members of the team with similar experience, or work to a lower standard (possibly resulting in complaints from colleagues, service users or other professionals). She may seem to find it difficult to make the simple day-to-day decisions about her work that one would expect a practitioner to make on her own, without constant direction. (If this is the case, the idea of the 'blocked cycle' from Wonnacott [2012] discussed in Chapter 2, p 31 may be relevant.) Some underperformers identify illness or other problems as the reason for the problems with their work, and of course this may well actually be the case, but the supervisor needs to avoid succumbing to the '*Treat me, don't beat me*' game if so.

NIPPING PROBLEMS IN THE BUD

Many chronic difficulties can be avoided by being careful and thorough at the early stages. In my experience, the problems that supervisors talk about on courses have often become intractable precisely because they were not addressed at an early stage, and may have been allowed to 'fester' more or less unchecked for long periods, sometimes for many years, probably because in the short term it always seems easier to postpone action than to take it. Yet this places a serious burden on the supervisor and the team as a whole, reduces the authority of the supervisor in the eyes of the team, and may deprive service users of the better service they might otherwise have had. In many cases, failure to act early is also unfair to the individual concerned, if it means that she has been allowed to struggle on, for a significant portion of her working life, in a job that she may not be suited for.

Careful recruitment

Some people have problems coping with their work because they are simply not suited – or at least are not yet ready in terms of their own personal development – to undertake the challenges it involves. Not everyone is a people person. Not everyone has the necessary analytical skills. Many do not have the emotional resilience and/or maturity to cope with the very high emotional demands of many human service roles. If so, it's in their own interests, as well as in the interests of human service organisations and their clients, for them to do something else.

The first stage at which would-be recruits for a profession can be redirected elsewhere is when they apply for training courses, and the admissions tutors and lecturers have a heavy responsibility as the first gateway into the profession. Some would argue that higher education doesn't always live up to this responsibility. In a study on the factors leading to failing nursing students, Kathleen Duffy found that lecturers and mentors felt that the priority in higher education was 'bums on seats', rather than high professional standards, as in the following comment by a participant: '*The university is bums on seats. And whenever a student is out and then appeals, 100% of the time they come back. The only ones that we really see the back of properly are the ones that choose to leave themselves*' (Duffy, 2003: 25. Italics in original).

A second gateway at which potentially unsuitable candidates for the work can be deflected is the practice placement. Here the principal gatekeeper is a supervisor, the practice educator, who supervises students on placement and decides whether their work is of an acceptable standard for a pass. But higher education institutions have a major role here too. Duffy cites studies that suggest that nursing mentors often feel unsupported when they think a student should not pass (2003: 49), and I'm aware of practice educators in social work who feel the same.

It is not just lack of support that makes it difficult to fail a student, though. Other factors include an awareness of the subjective nature of assessment – and in particular difficulties in objectively assessing qualities like 'attitude' or 'bedside manner' – fears about appeals and the protracted, painful battles that can ensue, and feelings of guilt or regret for the student (Elliott, 2016). Writing about the same issue in social work education, Johanna Finch writes that 'assessors find it difficult to fail students because of the intense feelings of anger, guilt, shame, stress and sense of internalised failure' (2009: 126).

A study on underperforming physiotherapy students identified a somewhat different problem, which is that clinical educators speak of underperformance as a 'diagnosis', and that this way of looking at it 'places the responsibility for the students' passing/failing firmly on the clinical educator in terms of identifying potential causes and strategies for curing the condition' (Bearman et al., 2013: 540). In a study of the impact on social worker practice educators' experiences of making the decision to fail a student, one practice educator said she had blamed herself: 'I thought it was me. I was thinking, It's me, clearly me. My style isn't working. My sense of irony or something' (Basnett and Sheffield, 2010: 2125). Another observed that the whole team blamed the practice educator: 'I felt that the team dynamics broke down very quickly. People sided with the student, and because the student was very manipulative, I was seen as the baddy' (Basnett and Sheffield, 2010: 2127).

These situations are very challenging for practice educators, particularly if they feel unsupported. (For more on the reasons for 'failing to fail' in nursing education see Finch [2009] or Docherty and Dieckmann [2015], and see Bachman et al. [2019], on the same problem in social work education.) Similar painful feelings – guilt, anger, shame, a sense of failure – will be present for a supervisor or manager embarking on disciplinary procedures in respect of a member of staff who is simply not up to the job.

However, when recruiting for a post in a team and deciding whether to appoint, the situation is much more straightforward, for here it is not a question of failing someone, but rather of deciding which, if any, of the candidates is best suited to the post. If the team is very busy, it can be tempting to appoint whoever is available, but to appoint a member of staff who is not really right for the job is, in the long run, likely to lead to far more problems than struggling along a little longer with a vacant post. *The recruitment process is the single best opportunity for a supervisor or manager to avoid long-term problems.*

Use of induction to set standards and expectations

A further stage at which performance issues can be addressed before they become a serious problem is during induction and the probationary period. I have already discussed this in the previous chapter (see p 136) and will not go over it here except to repeat that an authoritative induction does not just support new recruits but makes demands of them. If you have set out from the beginning the standards you expect the new recruit to work to, the probationary period is the ideal time to address performance problems and, if necesssary, decide that the recruit is not currently ready for the job they have taken on.

Use of supervision to model and promote good practice

Establishing a pattern from the beginning of proper, regular, in-depth supervision is a very important part of preventing problems from building up. It allows the supervisor to recognise what the supervisee finds difficult from an early stage and provides an opportunity to work on these areas of difficulty, and it creates an atmosphere within which it is possible to discuss aspects of practice which need to be improved without this feeling like a sudden and unexpected blow. Specifically, supervision in which supervisee and supervisor 'games' are resisted (see Chapter 7) will help to prevent a number of the problems discussed above, several of which, as I've already noted, are associated with, and may be inadvertently maintained by, 'games' such as '*Treat me, don't beat me*', or '*Two against the agency*'.

You will recall that there are two ways of tackling 'games'. The first is simply not to play them. The second is to name them. An experienced manager described three 'games' to me (although she didn't use that word) which, in her experience, can in particular be signs of trouble:

- Game 1. Supervisee has her own agenda which she does not disclose. (This is the game that Kadushin calls '*What you don't know won't hurt me*' [1999: 62].) This game is difficult to challenge if the agenda is *completely* hidden, but if the supervisor has any sense of something not being disclosed, the way to refuse to play is to be very persistent, and to continue to ask questions about the area where the supervisee appears to be hiding something, pushing for details, and asking for clarification of things that the supervisee seems to want to remain cloudy, until whatever has been hidden comes to light. The way to name the game is to say, 'There's something you're not telling me.'
- Game 2. Supervisee tries to turn supervision into a 'therapy session' (this is of course '*Treat me don't beat me*'). The way not to play is, having duly noted and sympathised with the supervisee's personal issues, to bring the discussion back to the supervisee's work. The way to name the game is to say something along the lines of, 'I understand that you are going through a difficult time, and I do sympathise, but right now I do still need to do my job of looking at your work. Perhaps you need to think about somewhere else to go to talk about your difficulties? I can put you in touch with the workplace counselling service.'
- Game 3. Supervisee introduces a steady stream of distractions, whether in the form of actual interruptions from outside of the meeting, or by constantly

changing the subject and mentioning things irrelevant to, or peripheral to, what is being discussed. The way not to play is to refuse to be distracted. The way to name the game is to say, 'I notice you keep taking phone calls. Can you please turn off your phone', or 'I notice you keep changing the subject. We don't have that much time, so can we please stick to our agenda.'

The following case study illustrates the first of those three 'games'.

Elspeth is a fairly experienced social worker. She is also a lone mother and has experienced poverty and domestic violence first hand. Her life has been pretty challenging at times. She knows she hasn't always been the best of parents in the past, but she and her children came through alright.

Elspeth trained as a social worker because she wanted to help people who struggled with the same sort of things that she struggled with herself. She is impatient with bureaucracy, and impatient with defensive, risk-averse practice. She thinks that the system is too quick to criticise and punish, too slow to encourage and support. She wants to be there for people as they try and turn their lives around, not just fill in assessment forms and go to meetings. She is considered by her peers to be very good at her job, and is very highly regarded by service users.

Elspeth has been working with a mother called Rhiannon who has been having some difficulties coping on her own, after extracting herself and her son Sean (aged 6) from a very abusive relationship. Rhiannon has been quite depressed, while Sean is agitated and restless, frequently refusing point blank to do as he is asked. Rhiannon has admitted that sometimes Sean pushes her to the end of her endurance, and at times she has felt close to hitting him. But she also, as she says, 'loves him to bits'.

On one of Elspeth's visits, during the summer holiday (which Rhiannon had anticipated would be a very challenging time), Sean came in while Elspeth was talking to Rhiannon, and Elspeth noticed that he had several quite pronounced hand-shaped marks on his leg, with marked bruising in several places to indicate that he was hit hard enough to break blood vessels under his skin. Clearly someone has completely lost it with him and slapped him repeatedly, pretty much as hard as they could.

'Okay,' says Rhiannon, 'before you ask, I smacked him. I was very tired, and he was being absolutely horrible. He started hitting me because he was angry I wouldn't buy him some sweets. I asked him to stop. I begged him to stop, in fact, but he wouldn't, and finally I lost my temper and smacked him way too hard. It won't happen again, but he was being awful and he knew it.'

Sean confirms this story. Elspeth is good with children and has an excellent relationship with him, and she has no sense at all of him being in any way cowed or intimidated by his mother. (And Elspeth knows what he's like when he's cowed: she has seen him with his stepdad.) Sean quite cheerfully acknowledges that he was being very naughty, that he was hitting his mother, and that she warned him to stop or she would smack him. The two of them seem very relaxed in each other's company now.

Elspeth makes it clear to Rhiannon that it's unacceptable to hit him like this, though actually she feels she hardly needs to say this, because Rhiannon has told her more than once that she strongly disagrees with corporal punishment of any kind, to the point that she's actually had arguments with several friends and neighbours who regularly smack their kids. Elspeth tells her she doesn't want to make too big a thing out of this if it really is a one-off incident, but that she will have to discuss it with her manager, and that she will let her know what her manager thinks. For the rest of the session, she goes back to the issues she's been working on with Rhiannon: sorting out debts and other practical problems, setting clear and consistent boundaries for Sean, building up a network for herself in her new neighbourhood.

As Elspeth drives back to the office, she struggles with what she is going to do about this. She has a new manager, who she hasn't yet got to know but has a reputation as a bit of stickler for the rules. This will be the first time Elspeth has discussed a case of this kind with her. She's afraid that the manager will insist that she takes this incident down the full formal child protection route – a case conference, the police, a child protection plan – and in her opinion this would be the last thing that either Rhiannon or Sean need, when they are just beginning to turn a corner. It could really knock Rhiannon's confidence right back, Elspeth thinks, and that wouldn't be good for Sean either.

Eventually she decides that she'll downplay the incident. It would be wrong to conceal the fact that Rhiannon slapped Sean, but she will allow herself a little bit of licence.

And so, in her talk with her manager about this case, she emphasises the following, all of which she believes to be true:

- Rhiannon is turning a corner, she is making constructive use of support from Elspeth and other services, she is coming out of depression.
- Sean is a handful and drives his mother to distraction at times, but he is very much loved by her.
- Sean is a bright boy, has a lot of personal charm, and has a lot going for him, as does his mother, who is also bright and able.

- Rhiannon is starting to manage Sean in a more consistent way, and he is beginning to calm down; both of them are in an entirely different place from where they were when Elspeth took the case on.
- This was an isolated incident, which Rhiannon herself admitted to, in which she eventually slapped Sean round the legs when he'd been hitting her repeatedly. This was out of character – Rhiannon doesn't believe in corporal punishment – and Elspeth is confident that she won't do it again.
- Elspeth spoke to Sean about this, who confirmed Rhiannon's story. This is a loved child, who knows he is loved, and an able, basically responsible mother who has been through a very hard time.

Asked about the injuries to Sean, Elspeth confirms that she saw a red mark consistent with a recent smack, but does not mention the bruising, and does not share her private opinion that Rhiannon must have hit him pretty much as hard as she could. Elspeth's agenda for the supervision session is to avoid at all costs a 'heavy handed' child protection response to this incident, and so she withholds information, though she would be uncomfortable telling an outright lie.

EXERCISE 9.2

Extracting information from a supervisee who is holding back

The above is a very different scenario from the case of Godfrey in Chapter 5 (p 83), who felt intimidated by the father of a possibly abused child, and whose agenda was to avoid having to go back and meet this family ever again. Elspeth is a confident worker, has a good working relationship with Rhiannon and Sean, and may well be doing a very good job with them in many respects, but she is withholding important information which her manager ought to know. This is maverick behaviour which undermines the supervisory relationship.

If you were Elspeth's supervisor, clearly you would not know what you have just read above. But how might you detect the presence of a hidden agenda and undisclosed information? And how might you prise this missing information out of her?

It's possible that you wouldn't detect it, which would be Elspeth's responsibility. However, I have had students perform role plays based on this scenario over a number of years and those playing the supervisors normally do manage to detect that Elspeth is avoiding talking about something, and do eventually prise it out of her. It is often possible to tell that someone is trying to skate quickly over a topic that makes them uncomfortable – in this case, the topic of what precisely she saw in terms of injuries – and, having noticed that, to refuse to move on, decline to accept the various 'games' that the supervisee may try to play, and persist in asking questions until the full story emerges. Most people are more uncomfortable about telling a direct lie than they are about 'being economical with the truth'. Very direct questioning would put Elspeth in a position where she would have no choice but to reveal what it is she is trying to avoid talking about, unless she was prepared to lie. It would also be possible actually to say to Elspeth, 'It feels like you don't want to talk about this, why is that?' or 'I get a sense that there's something you're not telling me'.

Recording

Suppose in the above example, Elspeth persisted in refusing to reveal that she had seen bruising. And suppose you, as her supervisor, recorded what she did tell you, and she saw and agreed to your record – she should of course have also recorded what she saw on Sean's file – but it subsequently came out that (say) another professional had also seen the bruises that day, you would have evidence that Elspeth had not been honest with you. This would be valuable for future work with her.

Clear recording of the key points discussed in supervision, and particularly of actions that both parties have agreed to complete within a given timescale, are always important in supervision, as in any business-like meeting, so that future meetings can build on what has already been agreed. But it is particularly important that any discussions about performance issues are recorded by the supervisor – and the record shared with the supervisee – even when it isn't yet apparent that they are likely to become a long-term problem.

It is not fair to suddenly challenge a behaviour which you have apparently been willing to tolerate without comment for a long time, but memories are imperfect and also selective, and just raising a concern orally is not enough. Only if the supervisor has a record of the discussion whose accuracy was agreed at the time by both parties, can the supervisor demonstrate (if this is indeed the case) that the issue has been raised and discussed in the past. And the record provides a safeguard for the supervisee also, if in fact the supervisor's recollection is not correct.

AVOIDING BECOMING PART OF THE PROBLEM

It is not uncommon for the supervisor to be, without knowing it, part of the problem.

Head in the sand

I have already discussed how problems can become entrenched, and hard to undo, if they have been left unchallenged for a long time (or if they have been challenged, but ineffectively so, and there is no record of this having happened). It is much easier in the short run, to work round a staff member who does not pull her weight, than to embark on the time-consuming and painful process of doing something about it. It is easier to allow licence to mavericks for the same reason, even if this results in resentment from other team members who 'play by the rules'. I have been guilty in the past of 'sticking my head in the sand' about performance issues, like many supervisors, but it is a kind of dereliction of duty to adopt this approach, and the cost in the long run can be huge.

Set-up-to-fail syndrome

I discussed the 'set-up-to-fail syndrome' (Manzoni and Barsoux, 1998, 2002) in Chapter 4 (see p 62). This occurs when a supervisor decides that a member of her team is underperforming in some way. It begins when some triggering event, which 'sows a doubt in the boss's mind, and the boss begins to worry that the employee's performance may not be up to par' (Manzoni and Barsoux, 2002: 6). The supervisor then begins to micro-manage that employee. Supervisees who are being micro-managed become aware that they are being treated differently from others, and that the manager does not trust them or have confidence in them, and their behaviour begins to change:

> Deprived of elbowroom, they start to doubt their own thinking and ability, and they lose the motivation to make autonomous decisions. Feeling second-guessed much of the time, they figure, 'Why should I take risks when the boss won't appreciate it anyway?' Or else they hunker down and get on with the job but try to steer clear of the boss. (Manzoni and Barsoux, 2002: 6)

The whole pattern is aggravated by the human tendency to interpret what we see through the lens of what we think we already know. This is known to psychologists as 'confirmation bias' (I discussed it in Chapter 5, p 75), but is also the basis of the sociological idea of 'labelling'. Manzoni and Barsoux do not explicitly refer to it, but Howard Becker's influential book, *Outsiders* (1997), first published in the 1960s, showed how a 'deviant' label (such as 'young offender') can easily become self-perpetuating, so that the deviant behaviour becomes more entrenched as a result of professional intervention than it might otherwise have been.

In the same way Manzoni and Barsoux demonstrate that, once a supervisee has been labelled as a problem, everything she does may be interpreted in a completely different way from how the exact same action would be understood if performed by another employee, to the point where, 'quite conceivably ... a similar set of behaviors will lead one person to be labeled a model employee and another to be labeled a "political animal"' (2002: 82) who is just trying to 'make himself or herself look good' (2002: 83). Readers with a social work background, or a background in youth work, youth offending work, or teaching, may be familiar with the way this kind of process can easily happen with service users: once she has been negatively labelled, even improvements in the behaviour of the service user may be viewed with scepticism and suspicion. And of course, if improvements in behaviour bring no recognition, there is no incentive to maintain them.

More more more

In 'set-up-to-fail syndrome' the supervisor makes it difficult for the staff member to move forward, or to demonstrate that she has moved forward, by an overly negative or punitive approach which doesn't leave room for change. So the supervisor erroneously locates the whole problem within the supervisee, when in fact she, the supervisor, may be perpetuating the problem herself. However, an opposite pattern exists in which the supervisor takes on the failings of a supervisee as if they were her own. I have already discussed how practice educators can make this mistake (the example came from physiotherapy education) by taking full responsibility for the problem, as if the student were ill and they were the doctor providing treatment. As a result, the 'response to a failing student was to provide "more more more" rather than to engage in structured and directed support. If participants are failing to progress, then by doing "more" the clinical educator will "get them over the line"' (Bearman et al., 2013: 540).

This same pattern can unfold between managers and staff as well as between educators and students. In fact this behaviour is precisely what supervisors will inevitably fall into if the supervisee (probably unconsciously) is able to persuade them to play the game '*Treat me, don't beat me*' (Kadushin, 1999). In extreme versions of the pattern, the supervisee's failure becomes the *supervisor's* failure to the point that, if the supervisor fails to fix the problem, it is the supervisor who is letting the supervisee down, rather than the other way round.

Sometimes practitioners behave in a similar way with service users, by taking on more responsibility for solving their problems than is realistic, and forgetting that service users do have responsibility for their own lives and choices. (Inexperienced practitioners who are not that confident that they have anything to offer, may be particularly prone to this mistake.)

Being authoritative

This brings me back to Baumrind's parenting styles (1978) which (following Wonnacott, 2012) I used in both Chapter 4 and Chapter 8 to provide an analogy for different supervision styles (see pp 56 and 139). Figure 9.1 extends this analogy to different ways of responding to performance issues. The 'head in the sand' approach is neglectful: it simply doesn't address the problem at all. The 'set-up-to-fail' approach is authoritarian: it is strong on demandingness, but weak on responsiveness. The 'more more more' approach is permissive: it is strong on responsiveness, like an indulgent parent, but weak on demandingness. The best approach is authoritative, which involves being both demanding and responsive, offering support, but ultimately placing responsibility for change on the supervisee.

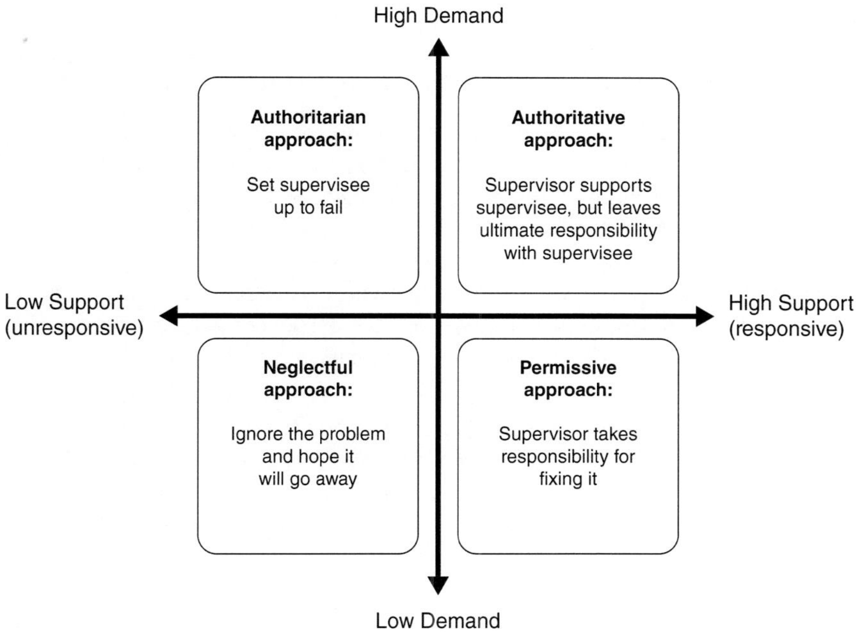

Figure 9.1 Approaches to performance issues using the analogy of Baumrind's (1978) parenting styles

CONCLUDING NOTES FOR SUPERVISORS AND SUPERVISEES

Notes for supervisors (including practice educators)

The problems discussed in this chapter are particularly difficult ones for supervisors, and I wish I was able to offer more straightforward solutions. What I have done in this chapter is, firstly, suggest ways of preventing these problems building up, through careful recruitment, authoritative induction of new staff, and thorough, authoritative supervision that declines 'games'.

(Continued)

Dealing with problems that have already become entrenched is much more difficult, but I have identified several ways in which supervisors can inadvertently perpetuate problems, specifically the 'head in the sand' approach, the 'set-up-to-fail syndrome' and what I called the 'more more more' approach in which the supervisor takes sole responsibility for fixing the problem, rather than being clear with the supervisee about what is her responsibility.

Clear records of the content of supervision sessions and the decisions made is extremely important, because disputes are likely about what was said and agreed.

Notes for supervisees (including students on placement)

This chapter is a reminder that supervisors are not just there to look after their supervisees (though they certainly have a duty of care), but also have a responsibility to the organisation, service users and other members of their team, to challenge supervisees on poor performance. (Practice educators in addition have a duty to the profession and its standards.) You cannot expect supervisors to place loyalty to their supervisees above these other competing claims. However, you *should* expect supervisors to try and understand difficulties you are having with the job, and – without becoming your therapist or counsellor – to provide you with support in overcoming them.

This is not, however, a 'them' and 'us' issue, since members of a team typically look to their supervisor to address problems that are caused for the whole team by colleagues who are not 'pulling their weight' or are in other ways making it harder for them to do their job. You may well find yourself in situations where you wonder why your manager is not doing more to (say) challenge a team colleague who is always late, or one who never seems to agree to take on a new case.

CHAPTER SUMMARY

This chapter looked at problems that have to be addressed in supervision and identified several common types of problem which create serious difficulties for supervisors, team colleagues, and the individuals concerned. It emphasised the importance of addressing potential problems early through recruitment, induction, good supervision and good recording practice.

It also used the analogy of the parenting style model discussed in previous chapters to look at different approaches to these problems – neglectful, authoritarian, permissive and authoritative – suggesting that the first three approaches are all likely to aggravate or entrench the problem rather than resolve it.

Addressing these kinds of problems can be among the most stressful things that supervisors have to do, but they are certainly not the only stressful things that supervisors deal with, and in the next and final chapter, I will look at how supervisors look after themselves.

10

THE NEEDS OF THE SUPERVISOR

CONTENTS

Some years after I finished being a team manager and became a lecturer, I ran into someone who had been the team manager of an adjoining team to my own. She had also moved on to other things and we reminisced for a while about the work we both used to do. At a certain point I asked 'Is it just me, Gill, or is this conversation making you feel very anxious?' She said she felt exactly the same. Even just the memory of the job, it seemed, was sufficient to make us both feel quite stressed. (I think in my case the single most stressful aspect was constantly juggling my awareness that my supervisees had too much to do, with my awareness of new work coming in that badly needed allocating.)

The point of telling this story is to validate the feeling of many supervisors that they are doing a very difficult job. Many, like me and my former colleague, are also managers, and have other responsibilities than simply supervision (responsibilities for unallocated work, responsibilities to provide data for senior managers, and sometimes financial responsibilities too). Some are still practitioners but with additional supervisory responsibilities (which are always to some degree *managerial* responsibilities). Some are practice educators who may have no formal managerial responsibilities, but they do, as discussed in the previous chapter, have the very challenging task of determining whether a student's work reaches the standard for a pass.

THE TRANSITION TO MANAGEMENT

Although not all supervisors are managers, all to varying degrees have moved to a position of authority over members of their own profession (or aspiring members of their own profession in the case of practice educators) who would previously have simply been colleagues. All have new roles and responsibilities which require an adjustment in self-image. Supervisors of practitioners have a unique 'middle' position in the organisation, facing in two different directions: towards practice (their own former milieu) in one direction, and in the other towards management with its very different demands and priorities. David Sims (2003) suggest that middle managers struggle with the fact that they must tell somewhat different 'stories' depending on which way they are facing, and that this in itself creates psychological tension. But 'middles' must deal also with the fact that they have made themselves different from those who used to form their peer group and must now preserve a certain professional distance from former colleagues in order to be able to exercise authority and to be seen as impartial. There is a loneliness in this, which can lead to what Carolyn Cousins (2010) called 'games of abdication' as discussed in Chapter 7. In addition, they must take responsibility, no longer just for work that they perform themselves, but for a much larger body of work which mostly takes place when they aren't even there, and which they can only understand and control to the extent that they are able to establish the solid supervisory relationship with their supervisees that has been the subject of this book.

In order to make a success of this, those who move from practice to become supervisors or managers need to relinquish a certain idea of themselves that accompanied their former role and construct a new and different way of seeing themselves, a transition which, until it is completed, can result in a feeling of interior conflict. Quite often the transition is accompanied with very little in the way of training. Writing about new nurse managers, Leah Curtin writes:

> It isn't that they are asked to do 'more' nursing or more expert nursing, or indeed any nursing at all. They have been put into a new job that requires a new set of skills, for which they are unprepared and usually left there. (Curtin, 2009: 25)

In strongly relationship-based professions like social work or youth work – professions in which, unlike in nursing, there isn't a substantial *technical* component to practice – there is a sense in which the transition to a management or supervisory role is akin to an earlier transition that we make when we move into a professional role, and learn that being a professional is a very different thing from being simply a friend, or a good neighbour. (In both cases, the shift involves learning to accept, and be comfortable with, authority.) But the shift involved is still a substantial one.

Assuming a supervisory role, and doing it authoritatively, requires courage, and it is not surprising that all of us fall short at least occasionally, in some of the ways that I have identified elsewhere in the book, including:

- Short-circuiting the supervisory cycle (see Chapters 2, 5 and 6)
- Adopting an over-controlling authoritarian 'style' or an over-indulgent permissive style – or even sometimes the neglectful approach of avoiding responsibility for aspects of the role altogether (see Chapter 4)
- Playing 'games' of power or abdication, or colluding with supervisee 'games' (see Chapter 7)
- Aligning too much either with practitioners or with management, to avoid the loneliness of the 'middle' position (see Chapter 8)
- Ducking the difficulties of challenging poor performance properly, whether by not dealing with it at all, or by setting up supervisees to fail, or by assuming too much responsibility for the practice shortcomings of others (see Chapter 9).

OWN SUPERVISION

The existence of supervisors is, of course, based on the assumption that people need supervision in order to do the best possible job. This doesn't magically cease to be true in the case of supervisors themselves. Just like their supervisees, supervisors are attempting to understand complex human situations, involving people about whom they will have the usual range of complicated feelings, but with the added twist that in their case there are two whole layers of 'Experience' (using the word in the sense explained in Chapter 2) that they need to try and get a grasp of. The first layer consists of the world of their supervisees. The second layer consists of the world of service users which, in many or most cases, they largely rely on their supervisees to tell them about. So, just like their supervisees, 'supervisors need training and good supervision for themselves in order to continue to grow in their practice' (Davys and Beddoe, 2010: 107).

The reality for supervisors and for practitioners alike is that the supervision that is actually available is not always what one would hope for. Supervisors will normally answer to more senior managers who are a further step away from direct practice, and this can feel like a limitation. Supervisors should ask for the supervision they need, but, just as practitioners sometimes have to do, they may also have to look for other kinds of support.

IMPORTANCE OF PEER GROUP

The meeting with the former colleague with which I began this chapter, was a reminder to me of the importance of the peer group as a source of support for supervisors and 'middles' in general. The middle position is a lonely one because to do it well you must resist the temptation to play *'I'm really one of you'* in relation to your supervisees (Delano and Shah, 2006: 37), while at the same time declining to simply be the creature of more senior managers, whose needs and priorities are necessarily different to your own, and who, preoccupied with their own concerns as they are, sometimes seem unaware of the precarity of the middle position:

> Middle managers suffer the double ignominy of having to create a sensible story to protect those who work for them from meaninglessness, and then trying to protect those same people again when the sensible story is suddenly turned into nonsense by their own managers.
>
> Meanwhile, [senior managers] ... often seem to be quite unaware of the ways in which they undermine their subordinates' storying ... (Sims, 2003: 1196–7)

The one group of people that does understand your own position is of course your peer group: those who are in the same position and doing the same job. If you are managing a team, there can sometimes be a sense in which those doing the equivalent job in other teams or units are your rivals in that they may compete with you for resources, or for the attention of senior managers, but nevertheless, your peer group do understand better than anyone else the unique challenges of your role. Building relationships, both individually and collectively, with other supervisors in the same position as yourself can be crucial to establishing a network that will provide support and be somewhere to turn to if you need to talk something over, whether you are a practice educator struggling with an underperforming student, or a team manager attempting to keep on top of new referrals with three staff vacancies in the team.

CONCLUDING NOTES FOR SUPERVISORS AND SUPERVISEES

Notes for supervisors (including practice educators)

The point of this very brief chapter has been to acknowledge that your needs are much the same as those of your supervisees. Like them you are attempting to make sense of highly complex and emotive situations, and like them you will often have difficulty in separating 'the wood from the trees'. The position of a supervisor can be a lonely one, and can entail making very difficult and painful decisions. You are entitled to expect supervision, just as your supervisees are, and should not be made to feel that it is a luxury or a weakness. But supervision may not meet all your needs for support, and it's important also to establish mutual support systems with your peers.

Notes for supervisees (including students on placement)

This chapter has been pitched at the needs of supervisors rather than supervisees. Supervisors offer many benefits to their supervisees – someone to share difficult decisions with, someone with a bit of detachment who will help you get a clearer perspective – but the point of this chapter has been that supervisors are only human, and have similar needs to those of their supervisees. This is something that is important to remember. Supervisees do have a part to play it making it possible for supervisors to do their job.

CHAPTER SUMMARY

This has been a very short chapter which concludes the book by pointing out that everything that has been said in previous chapters about the needs of supervisees applies equally to supervisors.

After briefly discussing the particular challenges of being a supervisor, in whatever role, and the particular challenges of being a 'middle manager' – the challenges unique to being a practice teacher were touched on in the previous chapter – I have mentioned the supervision needs of supervisors, and the importance of the peer group as a resource to provide general support and, where necessary, specific advice.

REFERENCES

Bachman, L., Groenvik, C., Hauge, K. and Julnes, S. (2019) 'Failing to fail nursing students among mentors: A confirmatory factor analysis of the Failing to Fail scale'. *Nursing Open*, 6(3), pp 966–73. Available at: https://doi.org/10.1002/nop2.276 (Accessed March 2020).

Basnett, F. and Sheffield, D. (2010) 'The impact of social work student failure upon practice educators'. *British Journal of Social Work*, 40(7), pp 2119–36.

Baumrind, D. (1978) 'Parental disciplinary patterns and social competence in children'. *Youth and Society*, 9(3), pp 239–76.

BBC (2018) 'Pte Sean Benton: Deepcut soldier's death was suicide, coroner rules'. Available at: www.bbc.co.uk/news/uk-england-44860108 (Accessed March 2020).

Bearman, M., Molloy, E., Ajjawi, R. and Keating, J. (2013) '"Is there a Plan B?": Clinical educators supporting underperforming students in practice settings'. *Teaching in Higher Education*, 18(5), pp 531–44.

Becker, H. (1997 [1966]) *Outsiders: Studies in the Sociology of Deviance*. New York: The Free Press.

Beckett, C. and Dickens, J. (2014) 'Delay and anxiety in care proceedings: Grounds for hope?' *Journal of Social Work Practice*, 28(3), pp 371–82.

Beckett, C. and Horner, N. (2015) *Essential Theory for Social Work Practice*, 2nd ed. London: Sage.

Beckett, C. and McKeigue, B. (2003) 'Children in limbo: Cases where court decisions have taken two years or more'. *Adoption and Fostering*, 27(3), pp 31–40.

Beddoe, L. and Davys, A. (2008) 'Revitalising supervision education through stories of confirmation and difference: The case for interprofessional learning'. *Social Work Now*, 40, pp 34–41.

Berne, E. (2016 [1964]) *Games People Play: The Psychology of Human Relationships*. London: Penguin.

Bogo, M. and Dill, K. (2008) 'Walking the tightrope: Using power and authority in child welfare supervision'. *Child Welfare*, 87(6), pp 141–57.

Bourn, D. and Hafford-Letchfield, T. (2011) 'The role of social work professional supervision in conditions of uncertainty'. *The International Journal of Knowledge, Culture and Change Management*, 10(9), pp 41–56.

Bowins, B. (2004) 'Psychological defense mechanisms: A new perspective'. *American Journal of Psychoanalysis*, 64(1), pp 1–26.

Bridge Consultancy (1997) *Report on professional judgments and accountability in relation to work with the Neave family*. Cambridge: Cambridgeshire County Council.

Brooker, C. and Repper, J. (2009) *Mental Health: From Policy to Practice*. London: Elsevier.

Brown, D. (2007) *Tricks of the Mind*. London: Channel 4 Books.

Burke, W. (2011) *Organization Change: Theory and Practice*, 3rd ed. London: Sage.

Carr, A. (1989) 'Countertransference to families where child abuse has occurred'. *Journal of Family Therapy*, 11(1), pp 87–97. Available at: https://onlinelibrary.wiley.com/doi/abs/10.1046/j..1989.00335.x (Accessed March 2020).

Constant, H. (2017) 'Five common mistakes social work managers should avoid'. *Community Care*, 12 April. Available at: www.communitycare.co.uk/2017/04/12/five-common-mistakes-social-work-managers-avoid/ (Accessed March 2020).

Cousins, C. (2010) '"Treat me don't beat me": Exploring supervisory games and their effect on poor performance management'. *Practice: Social Work in Action*, 22(5), pp 281–92. Available at: www.tandfonline.com/doi/pdf/10.1080/09503153.2010.514044 (Accessed February 2020).

Crenshaw, K. (1989) 'Demarginalising the Intersection of Race and Sex: A Black Feminist Critique of Intersection Doctrine, Feminist Theory and Antiracist Politics. University of Chicago Legal Forum 1989 (1), pp 139–67.

Curtin, L. (2009) 'Nursing management: Confounding the set-up-to-fail syndrome'. *Nurse Leader*, June, pp 24–8.

Davys, A. and Beddoe, L. (2010) *Best Practice in Professional Supervision*. London: Jessica Kingsley.

Delano, F. and Shah, J. (2006) 'Professionally packaging your power in the supervisory relationship'. *Scottish Journal of Residential Child Care*, 5(2), pp 34–44.

Delano, F. and Shah, J. (2011) 'Games played in the supervisory relationship: The modern version'. *Relational Child and Youth Care Practice* 24(1), pp 177–85. Available at: www.professionalpackagetraining.com/PPDocs/Games.pdf (Accessed February 2020).

Department for Education (DfE) (2015) *Social Work Knowledge and Skills for Supervisors and Leaders*. Available at: www.gov.uk/government/consultations/social-work-knowledge-and-skills-for-supervisors-and-leaders (Accessed September 2019).

Department for Education (DfE) (2018) *Knowledge and Skills Statement for Child and Family Practice Supervisors*. Available at: https://assets.publishing.service.gov.uk/government/uploads/system/uploads/attachment_data/file/708705/Post-qualifying_standard-KSS_for_child_and_family_practice_supervisors.pdf (Accessed September 2019).

Docherty, A. and Dieckmann, N. (2015) 'Is there evidence of failing to fail in our schools of nursing?' *Nursing Education Perspectives*, July/August, pp 226–31.

Duffy, K. (2003) *Failing Students: A Qualitative Study of Factors That Influence the Decisions Regarding Assessment of Students' Competence in Practice.* Glasgow: Glasgow Caledonian University.

Elliott, C. (2016) 'Identifying and managing underperformance in nursing students'. *British Journal of Nursing*, 25(5), pp 250–5.

Finch, J. (2009) 'Can't Fail, Won't Fail: Why Practice Assessors Find it Difficult to Fail Social Work Students. A Qualitative Study of Practice Assessors' Experiences of Assessing Marginal or Failing Social Work Students'. *DPhil thesis, University of Sussex*. Available at: https://sro.sussex.ac.uk/id/eprint/2370/1/Finch%2C_Johanna_Louise.pdf (Accessed March 2020).

Ford, J., Ford, L. and D'Amelio, A. (2008) 'Resistance to change: The rest of the story'. *Academy of Management Review*, 33(2), pp 362–77.

French, J. and Raven, B. (1959) 'The bases of social power'. In *Studies in Social Power*, D. Cartwright (ed.), pp 150–67. Ann Arbor, MI: Institute for Social Research.

Gallop, L. and Hafford-Letchfield, T. (2012) *How to Become a Better Manager in Social Work and Social Care*. London: Jessica Kingsley.

Gibbons, S., Murphy, D. and Joseph, S. (2011) 'Countertransference and positive growth in social workers'. *Journal of Social Work Practice*, 25(1), pp 17–30.

Goffman, E. (1967) *Ritual Interaction*. New York: Anchor Books.

Goldstein, J., Freud, A. and Solnit, A. (1980) *Beyond the Best Interests of the Child*. London: Burnett Books.

Hawkins, P. and Shohet, R. (2012) *Supervision in the Helping Professions*, 4th ed. Maidenhead: McGraw-Hill.

Hawkins, P. and Smith, N. (2006) *Coaching, Mentoring and Organizational Consultancy: Supervision and Development*. Maidenhead: Open University Press.

Hawthorne, L. (1975) 'Games supervisors play'. *Social Work*, 20(3), pp 179–83.

Hay, J. (2009) *Working it Out at Work: Understanding Attitudes and Building Relationships*. Hertford: Sherwood Publications.

Herskovits, M. (1948) *Man and his Works*. New York: Knopf.

Houston, G. (1985) 'Group supervision of groupwork'. *Self and Society: European Journal of Humanistic Psychology*, 13(2), pp 64–6.

Howe, D. (2009) *A Brief Introduction to Social Work Theory*. London: Red Globe Press.

Hughes, L. and Pengelly, P. (1997) *Staff Supervision in a Turbulent Environment: Managing Process and Task in Front-Line Services*. London: Jessica Kingsley.

Ingram, R. (2013) 'Emotions, Social Work Practice and Supervision: An Uneasy Alliance?' *Journal of Social Work Practice*, 27(1), pp 5–19.

Ingram, R. (2015) 'Exploring emotions within formal and informal forums: Messages from social work practitioners'. *British Journal of Social Work*, 45, pp 896–913.

Jabri, M. (2012) *Managing Organizational Change*. Basingstoke: Palgrave Macmillan.

Janis, I. (1982) *Groupthink: Psychological Studies of Policy Decisions and Fiascos*, 2nd ed. Boston: Wadsworth.

Kadushin, A. (1976) *Supervision in Social Work*. New York: Columbia University Press.

Kadushin, A. (1999 [1967]) 'Games people play in supervision'. *Reflections: Narratives of Professional Helping*, 5(3), pp 55–64. Available at: https://reflectionsnarrativesofprofessionalhelping.org/index.php/Reflections/article/view/624 (Accessed February 2020).

Kadushin, A. and Harkness, D. (2014) *Supervision in Social Work*, 5th ed. New York: Columbia University Press.

Kahler, T. and Capers, H. (1974) 'The miniscript'. *Transactional Analysis Journal*, 4(1), pp 26–42.

Kahneman, D. (2011) *Thinking, Fast and Slow*. London: Penguin.

Karpman, S. (1968) 'Fairy tales and script drama analysis'. *Transactional Analysis Bulletin*, 7(26), pp 39–44.

Kolb, D.A. (1984) *Experiential Learning: Experience as the Source of Learning and Development*, Vol. 1. Englewood Cliffs, NJ: Prentice-Hall.

Kotter, J. (2007) 'Leading change: Why transformation efforts fail'. *Harvard Business Review*, January, pp 96–101.

Maclean, S. and Harrison, R. (2015) *Social Work Theory: A Straightforward Guide for Practice Educators and Placement Supervisors*, 2nd ed. Lichfield: Kirwin Maclean Associates.

Manzoni, J.-F. and Barsoux, J.-L. (1998) 'The "set-up-to-fail" syndrome'. *Harvard Business Review*, March–April. Available at: https://hbr.org/1998/03/the-set-up-to-fail-syndrome (Accessed January 2020).

Manzoni, J.-F. and Barsoux, J.-L. (2002) *The Set-Up-to-Fail Syndrome: How Good Managers Cause Great People to Fail*. Boston: Harvard Business School Press.

McKitterick, B. (2012) *Supervision*. Maidenhead: Open University Press/McGraw-Hill.

Menzies, I. [aka Menzies Lyth] (1960) 'A case-study in the functioning of social systems as a defence against anxiety: A report on a study of the nursing service of a general hospital'. *Human Relations*, 13, pp 95–121.

Menzies Lyth, I. (1988) *Containing Anxiety in Institutions: Selected Essays*, Vol. 1. London: Free Association Books.

Miller, W. and Rollnick, S. (2012) *Motivational Interviewing: Helping People Change*, 3rd ed. New York: Guilford Press.

Morrison, S. and Halpern, K. (2012) 'Supervision skills to enhance appraisals'. In *Supervision in Medical Settings*, D. Owen and R. Shohet (eds), pp 105–16. Maidenhead: Open University Press.

Morrison, T. (2005) *Staff Supervision in Social Care*. Harlow: Longman.

Myers, P., Hulks, S. and Wiggins, L. (2012) *Organizational Change: Perspectives on Theory and Practice*. Oxford: Oxford University Press.

Nittrouer, C., Hebl, M., Ashburn-Nardo, L., Trump-Steele, R., Lane, D. and Valian, V. (2018) 'Gender disparities in colloquium speakers at top universities.' *Proceedings of the National Academy of Sciences of the United States of America*, 115(1), pp 104–08.

Payne, G. (2013) *Social Divisions*, 3rd ed. London: Red Globe Press.

Payne, M. (2014) *Modern Social Work Theory*, 4th ed. London: Red Globe Press.

Plant, E. and Peruche, M. (2005) 'The consequences of race for police officers' response to criminal suspects'. *Psychological Science*, 16(3), pp 180–3.

Proctor, B. (1988) 'Supervision: A co-operative exercise in accountability'. In *Enabling and Ensuring: Supervision in Practice*, 2nd ed., M. Marken and M. Payne (eds), pp 21–34. Leicester: National Youth Bureau and Council for Education and Training in Youth and Community Work.

Richards, M., Payne, C. and Shepperd, A. (1990) *Staff Supervision in Child Protection Work*. London: National Institute of Social Work.

Ryde, J. (1997) *A Step Towards Understanding Culture in Relation to Psychotherapy*. Bath: Bath Centre for Psychotherapy and Counselling.

Saunders, S., Sim, J., Kingstone, T., Baker, S., Waterfield, J., Bartlam, B., Burroughs, H. and Jinks, C. (2018) 'Saturation in qualitative research: Exploring its conceptualization and operationalization'. *Quality & Quantity*, 52, pp 1893–1907.

Schön, D.A. (1983) *The Reflective Practitioner: How Professionals Think in Action*. New York: Basic Books.

Seldon, S. and Sowa, J. (2011) 'Performance management and appraisal in human service organizations: Management and staff perspectives'. *Public Personnel Management*, 40(3), pp 251–64.

Signs of Safety (n.d.) Available at: www.signsofsafety.net/signs-of-safety/ (Accessed September 2019).

Sims, D. (2003) 'Between the millstones: A narrative account of the vulnerability of middle managers'. *Human Relations*, 56(1), pp 1195–1211.

Svensson, K. (2009) 'Identity work through support and control'. *Ethics and Social Welfare*, 3(3), pp 234–48.

Taylor, H., Beckett, C. and McKeigue, B. (2008) 'Judgements of Solomon: Anxieties and defences of social workers involved in care proceedings'. *Child and Family Social Work*, 13(1), pp 23–31.

Turner-Daly, B. and Jack, G. (2017) 'Rhetoric vs. reality in social work supervision: The experiences of a group of child care social workers in England'. *Child and Family Social Work*, 22(1), pp 36–46.

Wikipedia (n.d.) 'The politician's syllogism'. Available at: https://en.wikipedia.org/wiki/Politician%27s_syllogism (Accessed March 2020).

Wilkins, D. (2017) 'How is supervision recorded in child and family social work? An analysis of 244 written records of formal supervision'. *Child and Family Social Work*, 22, pp 1130–40.

Wilkins, D. and Antonopoulou, V. (2019) 'What does supervision help with? A survey of 315 social workers in the UK'. *Practice*, 31(1), pp 21–40.

Wilkins, D., Forrester, D. and Grant, L. (2017) 'What happens in child and family social work supervision?' *Child and Family Social Work*, 22, pp 942–51.

Wonnacott, J. (2012) *Social Work Supervision*. London: Jessica Kingsley.

INDEX

FSC
www.fsc.org
MIX
Papier | Fördert gute Waldnutzung
FSC® C083411

Kolibri 360 GmbH
Ferdinand-Jühlke-Straße 7
99095 Erfurt, Deutschland
produktsicherheit@kolibri360.de